HOW TO PROFIT FROM READING ANN
HG4028.B2 L67 1993

DATE DUE

SE 16 '94	MY 1 00		
OC 28 '94			
MY 19 '95			
DE 8 '95			
MY 2 '97			
JE 5'01			

DEMCO 38-296

How To **PROFIT** From Reading **ANNUAL REPORT$**

Richard B. Loth

Dearborn
Financial Publishing, Inc.

While a great deal of care has been taken to provide accurate and current information, the ideas, suggestions, general principles and conclusions presented in this text are subject to local, state and federal laws and regulations, court cases and any revisions of same. The reader is thus urged to consult legal counsel regarding any points of law—this publication should not be used as a substitute for competent legal advice.

Publisher: Kathleen A. Welton
Associate Editor: Karen A. Christensen
Senior Project Editor: Jack L. Kiburz
Interior Design: Lucy Jenkins
Cover Design: N.S.G. Design

Published by Dearborn Financial Publishing, Inc.

Printed in the United States of America

93 94 95 10 9 8 7 6 5 4 3 2

Library of Congress Cataloging-in-Publication Data

Loth, Richard B.
   How to profit from reading annual reports / by Richard B. Loth.
      p. cm.
   Includes bibliographical references and index.
   ISBN 0-79310-240-5
   1. Corporation reports—United States. 2. Financial statements—
United States. 3. Line of business reporting—United States.
I. Title.
HG4028.B2L67 1993
808'.06665—dc20   92-23082
                                                                CIP

To Nancy, my loving wife and supportive life partner

ACKNOWLEDGMENTS

I have been fortunate throughout my life to have received valuable guidance and advice from numerous family members, friends and professional acquaintances. There is no question that my capacity for writing has been positively influenced by these experiences and relationships, which are respectfully acknowledged. My mother and father deserve special mention. Loving parents such as these are truly two of life's great gifts.

Three people deserve particular recognition for their roles in helping make the idea for this book a reality. I have grown accustomed to counting on my wife, Nancy, to provide countless hours of editing and critical comment to make what I write better reading. Her enthusiastic dedication to these tasks is evident throughout this book. Nancy's parents, John and Dorothea Langmaid, whose interest in my work has spawned a question-and-answer dialogue for several years, continuously restore my faith in the individual investor, the intended beneficiary of much of my writing. Their support and encouragement for this endeavor are gratefully recognized.

CONTENTS

LIST OF EXHIBITS

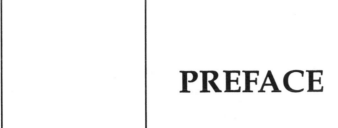

PREFACE

The yearly production and distribution of corporate annual reports in the United States is measured in the millions of copies. Averaging about 40 pages in size, the annual report is used by thousands of publicly held companies to communicate with their shareholders and a diversity of other users of annual report information. Among these users are employees, investment analysts and advisers, bankers, credit managers and members of the general public who are looking for a good place to work or to invest their savings. The corporate annual report is the single most practical way for these audiences to become informed about a company's financial condition and performance and to satisfy their particular corporate information needs.

While the effectiveness of the annual report's communication with these audiences often is questioned, reliable research continues to indicate that the annual report is an indispensable source of financial and investment information, particularly for individuals. If the annual report is the heart of corporate financial communications with the investing public, the public may be facing the financial reporting equivalent of cardiac arrest! American companies spend billions of dollars a year producing annual reports. The level of effort and cost is enormous, and troubling, because survey after survey indicates that a very large percentage of the readers of these annual reports, particularly the nonfinancial types, feel that annual reports are difficult to read, if not unintelligible.

Peter Lynch, the legendary ex-manager of the Fidelity Magellan Fund, provided this rather painful observation in his best-seller, *One Up On Wall Street*, which was aimed at the so-called average-investor audience: "It's no surprise why so many annual reports end up in the garbage can. The text on the glossy pages is the understandable part, and that's generally useless, and the numbers in the back are incomprehensible, and that's supposed to be important." While Lynch's remark may contain some literary hyperbole, it unfortunately reflects the views of many annual report readers. Such views rightly challenge preparers of annual reports to do better jobs.

Nevertheless, as business has become more complex, it is not surprising that corporate financial communications have paralleled this phenomenon. Financial professionals—public accountants, investment analysts and advisers, bankers and corporate financial managers—are major players when considering annual report presentations. They are the preparers and/or the critically important audiences for corporate annual reports, which have become the principal mediums used by companies to comply with the growing volume of required financial disclosure information.

This data can involve rather complex financial reporting. The professional investment community wants more detailed communication, which, as a consequence, contains more technical and lengthy explanatory language. The less-experienced annual report reader thus is faced with an increasing amount, and complexity, of unfamiliar jargon and accounting concepts in annual reports. It certainly would help the general public if the financial professionals worked harder at producing more readable, easy-to-understand documents.

While everyone is waiting for the corporate financial reporting millennium to arrive, where does all this leave those of you without a background in accounting or with only nominal financial know-how? Challenged! Just as the preparers of annual reports must strive to make the contents of their reports more user-friendly, inexperienced readers of annual reports must make a continuing effort to learn some of the basics employed by sophisticated financial analysts to discern a company's financial position and operating performance.

You do *not* need to become an accounting expert or a financial genius to fathom the complexities of annual reports. You *do* need to know what is important to look for in financial reports, where to find it and what it means to you as a user of corporate financial information. The objective of this book is to make complex financial reporting simple, or at least reasonably understandable for the nonfinancially oriented individual. You thus will be provided with the means to better understand a company's financial health. You will "profit" from these newfound skills in both your personal and professional financial decision making.

A few words of caution before proceeding further: First, the diversity of corporate activity and financial reporting practices associated with different businesses makes the task of preparing a single, definitive, comprehensive guide to understanding annual reports virtually impossible. For this reason, I have chosen to provide illustrations of representative elements of an annual report rather than examine an unrealistic, singular sample report. The material presented in this book relates to the vast majority of mainstream companies that are engaged in manufacturing, retailing, wholesaling and service businesses. While similar in some respects, the annual reports of financial institutions, insurance companies and public utilities are quite dissimilar with respect to the content and format of their financial statements and related information sections. Also, transportation and oil and gas companies each possess some unique characteristics that require forms of specialized financial disclosure. Therefore, for these special industry categories, the explanatory material and illustrations related to an annual report's financial information components will not be totally relevant.

Second, like members of other professional fields, those involved in financial reporting have developed a specialized language that often is incomprehensible to those readers without financial backgrounds. The financial novice may be turned off by this unfamiliar jargon and in too many cases may spend little or no time digesting the substantive information provided. This is unfortunate for both the preparers and the users of annual reports and represents a serious communications failure. I fear that the periodic annual report bashing that takes place in the financial press, which generally focuses on extreme cases of obfuscation, may someday lead to the following product warning labels on all annual reports: UNDIGESTED CORPORATE FINANCIAL REPORTING CAN BE HAZARDOUS TO YOUR WEALTH.

To avoid a similar situation from occurring here, this book contains a comprehensive, easy-to-understand glossary of annual report terminology. You are strongly encouraged to use this resource as you read through the book. In the *AAII Journal* (August 1991), Jean Henrich, assistant editor, appropriately notes that "numbers may play a prominent role in investing, but language remains key. Being well-versed in the standard terms and current slang can help in your understanding of financial and investment matters." If you want to grasp the meaning of financial reporting, you must develop a working knowledge of the *language*.

You now are ready to start your journey leading toward a better understanding of the information value of a corporate annual report. Just as important, I hope that *How To Profit from Reading Annual Reports* will prompt you to initiate a continuing interest in financial education and to apply this know-how to all your investing and professional activities.

1 THE ANATOMY OF AN ANNUAL REPORT

Broadly defined, the corporate annual report is a formal, detailed record of a company's financial condition and performance over a given period of time. It is issued yearly to shareholders, but it also is available to the general public, on request, usually three to four months after a company's fiscal year-end. The Securities and Exchange Commission (SEC) and the Financial Accounting Standards Board (FASB) set strict reporting and disclosure requirements for this document. After the debacle of the 1929 stock market crash, legislation (which also created the SEC) was enacted that set forth the requirements for the informational content of the annual report.

☐ CURRENT REGULATORY REQUIREMENTS

At present, the regulatory requirements of the annual report include the following items:

- Audited financial statements
- Quarterly financial data
- Five-year historical summary of financial data
- Description of the business
- Business segment information, if applicable
- Company directors and executive officers
- Two-year market price history of the company's stock and

- Management's discussion and analysis of the company's financial condition and the results of its operations

Since 1895, when the New York Stock Exchange first "recommended" that companies provide annual statements, the annual report has evolved into a major communications event. The influence of design, photography, graphics and printing techniques is readily seen in many of today's annual reports. The well-known investment adviser and writer, Thornton L. O'glove, has commented that "over the years public relations experts have gone to work to turn what was once a rather drab recitation of facts and numbers into what often appear akin to art books, more suited to the coffee table than the analyst's desk."

What you need to remember is that an annual report is nothing more than a glorified financial statement. There is nothing wrong with all the "gloss and glitter," especially if it encourages readership, but the information you need to know and analyze is concentrated in a few key sections of an annual report. I am not advocating a speed-reading approach or offering a quick and easy way to digest annual reports. The basic point to remember is that while all the information provided in an annual report is useful, some of it is more useful, and more critical, than other data. You therefore should set priorities as follows and proceed accordingly.

□ INFORMATION PRIORITIES

Before elaborating on this point, however, I must confess that I am an incurable annual report addict. I read them from cover to cover. I enjoy reading and discovering what some financial writers describe as the "mysteries" of this document. Very often what is not said, or reading between the lines, provides important insights into a company's financial condition and performance. I encourage you to do the same and intend to equip you, by the time you are finished reading this book, with the ability to interpret accurately what you see as well as what sometimes is absent.

The truth is that financial and investment analysis has a lot in common with the way a detective looks for clues to solve a case. Sometimes information turns up in the most unexpected places. Given a financial spin to his approach, television's popular detective, Columbo, would make a good analyst role model. He is thorough and patient and asks a lot of questions. You, like our fictional television hero, must set priorities and focus on solutions to a company's "financial mysteries."

Standardized Sections

While there is a great deal of variety in the presentation form of corporate annual reports, typically, you will find that they can be broken down into a number of fairly standardized sections. The content and sequence of appearance of these sections in an annual report are indicated in the following list of generally used sectional titles:

- Corporate Profile
- Financial Highlights
- Letter to the Shareholders
- Operational Overview
- Management's Discussion and Analysis
- Financial Statements
- Notes to Financial Statements
- Management's Report
- Independent Auditors' Report
- Historical Summary of Financial Data and
- Corporate Data and Shareholder Information

Order of Importance

The significance of each one of these parts of an annual report is dealt with in detail in the following chapters. What is important for you here, in this overview, is to recall my earlier comment about an annual report being a "glorified financial statement." Assuming you know what the company does, and if not, read the corporate profile, there are parts of the annual report that are more important than others, and they should be read in the following order:

1. Auditors' Report
2. Financial Statements and Notes to Financial Statements and
3. Management's Discussion and Analysis

Because these sections provide the critical data you need to judge a company's financial condition and performance, they constitute the heart of a corporate annual report.

Operational Overview

Next, you can proceed to the operational overview. While often emphasizing striking photography, impressive graphs and optimistic prose that supports a company's operations, this material can be informative, e.g., it can describe products and markets. Some companies do a better job of this than others. The same can be said for the historical summary of financial data, which, if done well, can provide a valuable long-term perspective on a company's financial position. In most instances, the financial highlights and the letter to the shareholders are given a definite company "spin" to support the performance of management. Few companies do a good job with these sections in terms of providing useful insights. Therefore, the information value is, unfortunately, only marginal at best. The corporate data and shareholder information sections contain items of a nonfinancial nature that often are useful, but can be read last. There is no need to read the management report. It is comforting, however, to see written down in black and white what you would naturally expect of a company's management.

In summary, concentrate your initial efforts at annual report reading on the core financial information provided in the sections indicated previously. Complement what you find there with additional input from the other parts of an annual report. The sequence of your review is important. There is a logical flow of events in the annual report review process, beginning with an assurance that the company's financial presentation is reliable, then having the availability of audited financial information to analyze and ending with unaudited, supplemental information on the company's activities and financial position.

2

AN INFORMATIONAL APPETIZER

☐ REVIEWING THE COMPANY INFORMATION AND FINANCIAL HIGHLIGHTS

Over the years, research on the habits of readers of annual reports indicates that, unfortunately, a majority of these individuals spend only a few minutes looking at the document before relegating it to a pile of "things to look at someday," or, just as likely, discarding it in the wastebasket. These readers most likely are going to focus, regrettably, on just the *appetizer*, because the annual report's informational *main course* is found elsewhere. Thus, vast numbers of annual report readers are getting only a taste of what they really need to know. This is not to say that the introductory information and financial highlights offer little value. Depending on a company's approach, the perspectives provided in this section can be quite useful. However, this data represents only a small portion of what you need to know if you are seriously interested in determining a company's financial and investment qualities. This, perhaps, should be the principal message you take with you after reading this chapter.

Generally, an annual report's *informational appetizer* consists of its cover presentation, a company profile, a mission statement of goals and objectives and a presentation of financial highlights. As I will repeat throughout the book, corporate practice varies greatly with regard to the content and format of the various components of an annual report. Those items not required by the Securities and Exchange Commission might not even appear. In the material presented here, the so-called mission statement is one such item that is not included with a great deal of frequency. However, as you will see from my following remarks, this may not be that great a loss.

☐ GETTING THE READERS' ATTENTION

The short attention span of the average annual report reader is precisely why preparers of annual reports so often emphasize the *packaging* aspects of the document. Graphic arts designers and their corporate clients often go to great lengths to create elaborate, eye-catching presentations. Even those companies with small annual report budgets and more conservative approaches want *nice* covers. In recent years, the corporate annual report has become, for many companies, just as important a marketing piece as it is a financial disclosure document. I like an annual report presentation that grabs my attention and makes me want to read what is inside. So my advice to you is this: Enjoy an annual report's glitz and glitter, but remember the old adage about judging a book by its cover.

I want to share with you, here, a few of my favorite annual report presentations for those of you who are not all that familiar with the subject. These examples give you some idea of the creativity and variety found in corporate annuals. My all-time favorite is actually a trio of annual report covers that illustrates how three different companies projected three very different images. Borrowing a line from an *Institutional Investor* article on this topic back in 1989, the approaches could be classified as "beefcake, cheesecake and apple pie." Respectively, Reebok International (1990) provided a 14-inch by 30-inch foldout cover of a male athlete, nude, except, of course, for the running shoes on his feet; the Dep Corporation (1988), a skin care products company, featured a tasteful, full-color photograph of a nude female on its cover; and the 1988 annual report cover of Energy North, a New Hampshire natural gas company, featured a homey scene of little children with a prominently displayed, handwritten recipe card for apple bread.

Other *packaging techniques* used to get the readers' attention include, among others, the traditional *smelly* annual report of McCormick, the spice company—the 1991 impregnated scent was whole Jamaica allspice. The America Business Products, Inc., 1986 annual came out, appropriately, in the form of a manila file folder, complete with tab and label. In similar fashion, Scanforms, Inc., a mailing forms manufacturer, created a realistic replica of the front of a metal mailbox for its 1987 report configuration. At the risk of revealing the author's food fixation, Pancho's Mexican Buffet, a restaurant chain, deserves special mention for its display of a delicious-looking plate of food spread over both the front and back covers of its 1987 annual report, which, because of the realism of the high-quality photograph, still makes me hungry.

Finally, the use of *slogans* on annual report covers can sometimes tip you off to what is inside. For example, the Perry Drug Stores 1987 annual offering carried the following message emblazoned from top to bottom on the front cover: "We have positioned the Company for renewal, transformation and revitalization in fiscal 1988. Our entire organization is dedicated to this goal." It was not surprising to find lots of red ink in the company's 1987 results, capping a three-year decline in earnings. Generally, phraseology of this nature sends a message to you before you even open up the annual report.

□ GETTING A FEEL FOR WHAT THE COMPANY DOES

Next, take a look at the company profile. As you can see in Exhibit 2.1, corporate practice can vary significantly. A concise but comprehensive description of a company's business is very useful to the reader, particularly if this is his or her first encounter with the company. This provides a basis for interpreting the company's operational and financial information that is found in the succeeding pages. What is the company's marketplace? What are its products/services or lines of business? How long has it been around? Is it a big or small operator? Where does it conduct its activities? A good profile will give you quick answers to these and other basic questions about the company.

□ THE *MOTHERHOOD* STATEMENT

Mission statements, in which companies generally make succinct expressions of their goals and objectives, principally aimed at investors, have become popular with investor relations and financial communications practitioners. As David Drobis, President of Ketchum Public Relations, states in the *Public Relations Quarterly* (Fall, 1991):

> If you glance through a random selection of annual reports, you'll see that many companies—perhaps most—substitute wishful thinking for explicit strategy. They aspire to be leaders in their markets.

EXHIBIT 2.1 Examples of Company Profiles

AMP INCORPORATED (1991 Annual Report)
AMP is the world leader in electrical/electronic connection devices, with a 17–18% market share in a $17–18 billion market.
Headquartered in Harrisburg, Pa., it employs 25,000 in 165 facilities in 31 countries. Well over 100,000 types and sizes of
terminals, splices connectors, cable and panel assemblies, net-
working assemblies, switches, electro-optic devices, touch
screen data entry systems and application tooling (54,000 ma-
chines); millions of tools are supplied to 200,000
electrical/electronic equipment makers—and tens of thousands of customers who install and maintain that equipment.

Virtually all growth was achieved by serving growth markets,
developing new products and entering new markets—acquisitions have not been a significant factor. Spending on research,
development and engineering for creation and application of
new and improved products and processes has been 9% of
sales for nearly 20 years.

Growth in the last 35 years from sales of $32 million in 1956
(when AMP became publicly owned) to $3.1 billion in 1991 (a
compound growth rate of 14%) has been directly linked to the
growth of the electronics (12–13%) and electrical/transporta-
tion (6–7%) equipment industries. In the last decade AMP's
annual sales growth rate slowed to 9.6% because of recessions,
industry corrections, slower market growth and price erosion.

PLY GEM INDUSTRIES, INC. (1990 Annual Report)
PLY GEM is a national manufacturer and distributor of spe-
cialty products for the home improvement industry. PLY
GEM's 10 independent operating subsidiaries are run by
excellent management teams employing 3,000 people in
60 locations throughout the U.S. and Canada. PLY GEM is
headquartered in New York City and its common stock &
convertible debentures are traded on the American Stock Exchange under the symbols PGI and PGI.A.

FIGGIE INTERNATIONAL, INC. (1990 Annual Report)
Figgie International, Inc., is a major diversified Fortune 500 operating company serving consumer, technical, industrial and
service markets worldwide.

Sources: Reprinted by permission of AMP Incorporated; PLY GEM Industries, Inc.;
and Figgie International, Inc.

They salute quality, value excellence, their customers and corporate responsibility; and they acknowledge that it's harder than ever to compete. The reports are invariably couched in forceful language, but there are few clues about where the companies are headed and how they intend to get there.

In my opinion, most of what I have seen in mission statements is, as Drobis describes, much like a *motherhood* statement. These generalized expressions of good intentions to do well as a business enterprise and act as a responsible corporate citizen are noble sentiments. If, however, quantifiable objectives are expressly stated, for example, target growth rates for sales and earnings, returns on equity and invested capital and debt ratios, these then become valuable benchmarks to judge management's performance over the years. If a mission statement is to be of any value, it must contain tangible objectives that are measurable.

□ FINANCIAL HIGHLIGHTS

The financial highlights section provides a condensed presentation of financial information and corporate data designed to give the reader a quick overview of a company's performance over the reporting period. The content varies considerably, but, in general, it contains quantitative information on sales/revenues, earnings, per-share figures, balance sheet items, financial ratios and other company information, often accompanied by supporting graphs. The financial highlights in Acme Steel Company's 1990 annual report are fairly representative of corporate practice (see Exhibit 2.2).

The information presented in the financial highlights generally has been carefully selected to put the company's financial condition and performance in the best possible light. There is not any evil motive here to deceive the reader. Certainly, companies are justified in putting their best foot forward. What users of this information need to know is that, without the details provided elsewhere in the annual report, many of the amounts and/or indicators appearing in this section often are not truly representative.

For example, impressive gains in net income may be the result of nonrecurring items that you will discover only by looking at the full income statement and reading the relevant notes. Dramatic sales increases may be caused more by acquisitions than improvements in volume from the preacquisition business base. In effect, there is nothing wrong with the numbers, but you must know how the numbers

EXHIBIT 2.2 Financial Highlights

ACME STEEL FINANCIAL HIGHLIGHTS
(Figures in thousands, except per-share, employee and shareholder data)

	1990	*1989*	*% Change*
For the year:			
Net sales	$446,042	$439,412	+ 2
Gross profit margin	8.2%	11.8%	−31
Income before taxes	$ 9,388	$ 26,126	−64
Income tax provision	3,755	9,926	−62
Net income	5,633	16,200	−65
Net margin	1.3%	3.7%	−65
Capital expenditures	$ 28,604	$ 14,960	+91
Cash flow from operations	24,045	20,805	+16
Depreciation	13,031	12,031	+ 8
Average shares outstanding	5,356	5,393	− 1
Per common share:			
Net income	$1.05	$3.00	−65
Shareholders' equity	28.65	27.63	+ 4
At year-end:			
Shareholders' equity	$152,730	$147,106	+ 4
Return on equity	3.8%	11.6%	−67
Working capital	$ 69,838	$ 84,883	−18
Long-term debt	59,500	59,500	—
Debt/% of capitalization	28%	29%	− 3
Number of shareholders	8,900	9,500	− 6
Number of employees	2,900	3,000	− 3

Source: Acme Steel 1990 Annual Report. Reprinted by permission of Acme Steel Company.

were produced to get an accurate idea of a company's performance. Suffice it to say that significant other data appearing in different parts of the annual simply do not *fit* into this intentionally brief section. Finally, comparisons of only two years, which are what most companies present in their financial highlights, are too narrow a focus to have any real meaning. A mediocre year following a bad year will look great! Indicating the percentage change in an item, which is helpful, means very little unless at least three to five years are shown to reflect a trend.

If you find that a company omits the financial highlights section, it may have a good reason. Take the case of the Grow Group, Inc., a diversified manufacturer, which was experiencing a pronounced and steady decline in earnings during the 1985–87 period. For anyone following the company's progress in those years through its annual report communications, it was obvious that 1987 was a very bad year. When you opened the report to look at the financial highlights—they were not there! Fortunately, most companies report the bad news along with the good news. Sometimes you have to look for it, but at least it is reported.

In summary, the opening pages of an annual report offer useful but limited information. Be aware of the limitations of the introductory material and financial highlights and look for useful data in those presentations that are more complete. If this part of the annual report is the only part with which you are familiar, you need to read on to discover what you have been missing.

3

A WORD FROM TOP MANAGEMENT

☐ **LETTER TO THE SHAREHOLDERS**

This component of an annual report presents a message from the company's chairman of the board or the president, or sometimes both, to the shareholders. The letter usually is two or three pages long, and its style and content can vary greatly. Generally, the letter will cover a company's business activities for the fiscal year under review, its financial condition and performance and its prospects for the future. And most likely, it will contain an impressive photograph of the signatory or signatories.

As an informational source for helping to determine a company's financial and investment qualities, the letter to the shareholders is controversial. Many objective observers feel that in most cases this presentation is crafted as a public-relations masterpiece with little, if any, substantive information. As *Sid Cato's Newsletter on Annual Reports* stated a few years ago, "fewer than one of three CEOs . . . actually writes his own letter, cornerstone of the document."

In a more recent survey by this same newsletter, it categorized as "disappointing" the finding that only 35.9 percent of the respondent companies' CEOs were "involved in the actual writing—in whole or in part."

□ HARD TO BELIEVE EVERYTHING YOU READ

According to a widely used reference book, *Barron's Finance and Investment Handbook*, "in the many spoofs that have been written about corporate annual reports and their reputation for obfuscation, the least mercy has been reserved for the letter to the shareholders." Unfortunately, each year's corporate annual offerings will provide, without fail, any number of examples for critics to target. Three major examples include the following syndromes.

"Let's Not Face the Bad News" Syndrome

This popular syndrome is found in many letters. The Amax, Inc., 1989 letter to its shareholders begins with this encouraging, positive statement: "The past year was truly one of accomplishments." What follows is paragraph after paragraph of explanation of what went wrong as company sales were down, operating earnings were off and net income per share fell by half.

"Hollow Statement" Syndrome

Another problem area involves the "hollow statement" syndrome—using bold language that raises readers' expectations for some solid input but leaves the readers hanging. Chevron Chairman Kenneth T. Derr's comments in the company's 1990 annual report grabbed my attention with these remarks: "We measure our performance not against what we did last year, but against what our strongest competitor is doing. Our goal is to be, as our mission statement says, 'better than the best.'" It was very disappointing to dig into the annual report and find absolutely no comparative industry information whatsoever except for a small callout in the margin near the end of the report.

"Bold Statement" Syndrome

Finally, the "bold statement" syndrome award in 1986 should have been awarded to Ahmed and Charles Kafadar, chief executive officer (CEO) and chief operating office (COO), respectively, of the smallish (net sales $41 million) OEA, Inc., company in Denver, Colorado. The Kafadars ended their upbeat shareholders' letter by boldly declaring that "OEA's name is becoming a household word in the United States and abroad . . ." This was a little hard to believe, especially for a manufacturer of propellent and explosive-actuated devices for aircraft personnel escape mechanisms. How often is this business the subject of dinner table conversation or the local news? And they are talking worldwide?

These examples are, unfortunately, representative of some of the writing that creeps into the shareholders' letter and generates so much skepticism on the part of many readers of annual reports.

□ WHAT TO LOOK FOR

In a 1986 study sponsored by the Financial Executives Research Foundation, corporate executives considered the letter "to be the most important part of the annual report, especially for individual investors." The same survey, however, found that professional and nonprofessional investors alike ranked the letter 10th and 12th, respectively, out of 13 annual report sections when asked to judge this component's informational importance to them. Even so, do not let the perceived low utility value of the letter to the shareholders deter you from attempting to extract valuable insights from this material. The experts will tell you that you must read between the lines, as well as pay attention to what is not said, for clues on how well or how poorly a company is performing. Exhibit 3.1, excerpted from an article in the *Financial Analysts Journal*, provides some interesting perspectives regarding the shareholders' letter. The authors of the article, from which this exhibit has been reproduced, reached a tentative but interesting conclusion for annual report readers:

> Clearly, an analyst [or any annual report user] cannot rely exclusively on the president's letter [shareholders' letter] to forecast a company's stock price performance. However, automatic dismissal of the president's letter [shareholders' letter] may result in the loss of important signals. Presidents of high-performing companies tend to expect gains, and their letters convey those expectations. Presidents of low performers tend to discuss neither gains nor losses.

Furthermore, mention of imminent losses is associated with subsequent stock price declines, whereas expressions of confidence tend to be associated with subsequent increases in stock price.

There also are positive exceptions to the general rule of mediocre shareholder letter presentations. These will be recognized for their candid language and objective appraisals of a company's track record and future prospects. They will tell you why the company succeeded or failed to perform, and in the case of the latter, what the company is doing about it. As you improve your financial analysis skills, you will develop a feel for what makes sense. Look for specifics, the writer's sincerity, a discussion of industry and general economic conditions affecting the company, an analysis of the competition and tangible indicators of the future course of the business.

No discussion of the shareholders' letter would be complete without mentioning the thoughtful and entertaining letters produced by Warren Buffett, the well-known investor and CEO of Berkshire-Hathaway, Inc. He has been writing long, informal and highly informative letters to the shareholders of Berkshire-Hathaway for many years. You need not have any investment interest in the company to benefit from Buffett's masterpieces. I strongly suggest that you include his annual letter in your regular reading material for financial and investment education. To request a copy of the company's annual report, write: Berkshire-Hathaway, Inc., 1440 Kiewit Plaza, Omaha, NE 68131.

☐ WHAT TO LOOK OUT FOR!

Finally, having told you what to look for in a letter to the shareholders, you also should be aware of what to look out for! Among other phrases, the following warrant your particular attention. For example, Martin Kellman, in a humorous but informative article on annual reports that appeared in *Barron's* (May 13, 1991), wrote that "to an investor, no word is more chilling than 'challenging.' It means your company has lost your money, is losing more of it and will continue to lose it."* Having studied this phenomenon, Kellman warns that "if the C-word, in any form, appears three or more times in the front pages of an annual report [the shareholders' letter] or, worse yet, shows up on the cover, sell immediately. The 'challenge' is making

---

* Reprinted by permission of *Barron's*, © 1991 Dow Jones & Company, Inc. All Rights Reserved Worldwide.

EXHIBIT 3.1 The Language of the Shareholders' Letter

The following material has been excerpted from an article, "The President's Letter To Stockholders: A New Look," written by Dennis McConnell, John Haslem and Virginia Gibson, for the *Financial Analysts Journal*, September–October, 1986. The authors analyzed a sample of letters to the shareholders, employing a technique widely used in the social sciences referred to as "content analysis." An examination of 100 shareholders' letters identified nine recurring themes. The themes and the phrases and words used to express them are as follows:

1. **Confidence**. Confidence is commonly expressed using terms such as *confident, optimistic* and *certain.*

2. **Market Context**. Words and phrases used to address features of the market beyond the control of the firm include *economy, recession, inflation, housing starts* and *legislation.*

3. **Growth**. References to *rapidly expanding markets, improving sales trends* and *expanding market share* are used in discussing future growth.

4. **Statement of Strategic Plans**. Strategic plans are expressed in phrases such as *building a strong foundation, strengthening the organization* and *strong position.* Specific tactical plans for accomplishing these goals are rarely discussed.

5. **Changing Product Mix**. Potential new products or services are discussed in either general or specific terms.

6. **Imminent Losses**. Phrases such as *short-term losses* and *reductions in asset size* are used to discuss anticipated declines.

7. **Imminent Gains**. Reference to future *gains, increased profits* and *resumption/increase in dividends* are used when discussing expected positive returns to the corporation and shareholders.

8. **Positive References to the Years Ahead**. This variable represents optimism about the long-term future. Phrases used in discussing the long-term include *the decade ahead, next several years* and *future.*

9. **Positive References to the Forthcoming Year**. This variable represents optimism about the year ahead. Generally, these references are to a specific year (199x), or to the *upcoming year* or the *year ahead.*

Reprinted with permission.

people buy something they no longer want or that doesn't work at a price they cannot afford or are unwilling to pay. A challenge indeed." The exaggerated use of public relations–inspired terminology generally indicates substandard corporate performance.

More serious issues are involved when the word *restructuring* is employed. This is what management does after it has made one or possibly several bad mistakes regarding the company's investment of its resources, both human and financial. While restructuring can cover a multitude of sins, it is most often related to the *corrective* actions that companies take to divest themselves of losing businesses. Somewhat forgotten in this process is the fact that these dispositions very often represent previously heralded acquisitions! Obviously, this costs the company money, which you will see as a "restructuring charge" expense in the income statement. The language used to explain all this generally implies that the problems are behind the company. While this may be true, the workout difficulties related to a restructuring can have a lingering effect on the company's earnings and cash flow for an extended period of time.

A 1989 survey by the respected investor-relations firm, Hill & Knowlton, found that the increasing use, which we still see today, of the phrase *building shareholder value* was causing the term to be viewed with growing skepticism by the investment community. Both security analysts and individual investors were critical of companies for failing to provide specifics. In the case of the analysts, 62 percent characterized the term as "meaningless boilerplate" or "defensive" or that management was "worried about a takeover." Individual investors were a bit more kindly, but a significant 29 percent simply answered "don't know" when asked what *shareholder value* meant. Merely being in favor of shareholder value, without defining specifically how this concept can be measured, tells you very little about the company.

My parting advice to you in this chapter should be fairly obvious by now. Simply stated, approach the letter to the shareholders positively, but with an attitude of healthy skepticism. By understanding the letter's apparently inherent limitations, at least as shown by those produced by corporations up until now, you can place its financial and investment informational value in its proper perspective. In Chapter 2, I referred to the benefit of employing the tactics of an investigative detective to help readers look for clues to a company's "financial mysteries." The shareholders' letter is a very appropriate place to start applying these skills.

4 OPERATIONAL OVERVIEW

☐ READING THE OPERATIONAL OVERVIEW

In terms of the various informational components of an annual report, the operational overview is the easiest one for most nonprofessional readers to understand. It generally is well written in understandable language and is visually attractive. It contains the largest number of pages, but, ironically, all of this length does not necessarily translate into strength—at least in the context of discerning a company's financial performance and condition.

☐ PROSE, PHOTOGRAPHS AND GRAPHICS TELL THE COMPANY'S STORY

As this section's heading implies, a company's operational overview is public relations–oriented, designed to impress but not necessarily to inform objectively. It tells the company's story in the best possible way. Nevertheless, I usually have found this part of an annual report to be interesting and worthwhile reading. There are no secrets to interpreting its content. The only advice that I can offer is to use your common sense. If a company presents a comprehensive, insightful look at its overall operations, you obviously will come away with a better understanding of how it operates. If the presentation is heavy on generalities, light on graphics and poorly formatted, it is not going to be of much value to you. On the other hand, a well-prepared overview can help you put a company's financial position into perspective.

For example, larger companies with several lines of business are sometimes too complicated to understand. Many companies with this kind of operational complexity provide what is referred to as a company matrix that describes each business segment's products and markets and highlights some key financial data. I particularly liked the Philip Morris presentation in its 1990 annual report (see Exhibit 4.1). The Philip Morris, General Foods, Kraft, Oscar Mayer and Miller Brewing division products were shown as they appear in the stores. Condensed market position information and sales and operating income figures were provided for each operating division.

A number of techniques can enhance the telling of a company's story and can add to your knowledge of its operations. Always remember that this story is meant to convey as favorable an image of a company's activities as is possible. While this type of data is recognizably helpful, the source of substantive information to analyze a company's financial and investment qualities lies elsewhere. This basic premise, which you should commit to memory, leads to what informed observers of financial reporting practices consider the heart of the annual report— those sections dealing with the financials and, particularly, those dealing with the audited material. Therefore, the next chapters, 5 through 13, deserve your serious and concentrated attention.

EXHIBIT 4.1 Reproduction of Company Matrix

Source: Philip Morris 1990 Annual Report. Courtesy of Philip Morris Companies Inc. Photography by Chris Collins.

EXHIBIT 4.1 Reproduction of Company Matrix (continued)

Kraft General Foods Canada

With a host of popular Kraft General Foods retail brands and a large food-service business, KGF Canada is Canada's largest packaged foods company.

Millions	1990	1989
Operating Revenues	$1,327	$1,251
Operating Companies Income	$ 235	$ 187

Oscar Mayer Foods

Already the leader in luncheon meats and bacon, Oscar Mayer also markets hot dogs, Louis Rich turkey products, Louis Kemp seafood products, Claussen pickles, and new Lunchables and Lunch Breaks lunch combinations.

Millions	1990	1989
Operating Revenues	$2,520	$2,270
Operating Companies Income	$ 145	$ 168

Kraft General Foods Frozen Products

KGF Frozen Products, the largest frozen food manufacturer in the world, introduced Sealtest Free nonfat frozen desserts, Breyers frozen yogurt, Kraft Eating Right frozen entrees, and Budget Gourmet Light and Healthy Dinners in 1990.

Millions	1990	1989
Operating Revenues	$2,155	$2,103
Operating Companies Income	$ 169	$ 169

Kraft General Foods Commercial Products

KGF Commercial Products has two divisions. Kraft Foodservice is the second-largest foodservice distributor in the United States. Kraft Food Ingredients is the country's leading processor of edible oils.

Millions	1990	1989
Operating Revenues	$4,161	$3,861
Operating Companies Income	$ 118	$ 160

Miller Brewing Company

Miller is the second-largest brewer in the world. Miller markets four of the top ten beers in the U.S. market: Miller Lite, Miller High Life, Milwaukee's Best, and Miller Genuine Draft. Other brands include Sharp's, the country's leading non-alcoholic brew.

Millions	1990	1989
Operating Revenues	$3,534	$3,342
Operating Companies Income	$ 285	$ 226

Operating companies income is income before amortization of goodwill, unallocated corporate expenses and interest and other debt expense, net and in 1989, gain on sale of the company's equity investment in Rothmans International p.l.c. and restructuring of food operations.

5 MANAGEMENT'S PERSPECTIVE

☐ REVIEWING MANAGEMENT'S DISCUSSION AND ANALYSIS

The management's discussion and analysis section—financial professionals generally use the shorthand term, MD&A—is an important part of a company's annual report presentation. Its more formal title is Management's Discussion and Analysis of Financial Condition and Results of Operation or Analysis of Operations and Financial Condition, and often it is referred to simply as the Financial Review. In this part of an annual report, the management comments on three major aspects of a company's financial position: results of operations, capital resources and liquidity. The SEC made this information a corporate financial reporting requirement in the mid-1980s, and it has appeared in annual reports since that time. The information presented in this section is not audited. However, when this section is done well, a reader can obtain some valuable perspectives on a company's financial condition and performance. Even a somewhat perfunctory MD&A narrative still can provide useful information.

SEC Recommendations

In this regard, in May of 1989, the SEC, concerned that companies were tending toward mechanistic, numbers-oriented presentations on year-to-year financial statement changes as contents for their reports' MD&A sections, issued an interpretive release specifying the kind of disclosure it would like to see. In brief, the SEC recommended that companies provide narrative explanations of their financial positions, with emphases on their prospects for the future. This emphasis on prospective information is very important. As you will see in later chapters, a company's financials are historical presentations; and in the words of the SEC's interpretive release, "the MD&A is intended to give the investor [and other users of annual reports] an opportunity to look at the company through the eyes of management by providing both a short- and long-term analysis of the business of the company."

Unfortunately, as reported in a 1989 Hill & Knowlton survey, "many companies are failing to meet investors' needs with the MD&A sections of their annual reports." The ensuing years have shown little improvement in general corporate practice with this financial reporting item. However, many financial professionals regard the MD&A section as a disclosure tool of potentially great value. It can provide insight on a company's financial condition and performance that is simply not evident in the historical financial statements. Additional information of a prospective nature in the MD&A is extremely useful to annual report users. I would venture to say that if there is no significant improvement in overall corporate conduct regarding the breadth and depth of disclosure in the MD&A section, specific informational requirements may be mandated very shortly by the SEC.

In its April 2, 1992, edition, *The Wall Street Journal* reported on an SEC case against Caterpillar, Inc., for its lack of disclosure of certain prospective information in the company's MD&A sections of its 1990 annual and quarterly reports. The newspaper article states that "securities lawyers said the case—the first to focus solely on the management discussion—would significantly affect the thinking of corporate America."* A Washington lawyer, Richard Phillips, is quoted as saying that "this is going to create quite a stir in corporate circles. . . . This is an attempt by the SEC to put some teeth into the MD&A requirements, and I think has to make a lot of companies reexamine their approach to the MD&A."

---

* Reprinted by permission of *The Wall Street Journal,* © 1992 Dow Jones & Company, Inc. All Rights Reserved Worldwide.

□ PRESENTATION ASPECTS OF THE MD&A SECTION

No doubt, some companies do a better job than others when writing good analytical, forward-looking MD&A sections. Before indicating what you should be looking for, let me warn you about three problems concerning the format and content of the MD&A section that you may find limiting and/or inhibiting.

The "Blur Technique"

First, if an MD&A is done well, its qualitative analysis content will be high. A good presentation also will make it easier for the reader to understand, by utilizing tables and charts to present quantitative data that the MD&A narrative explains. It is not unusual, however, to find all of the MD&A text run together, with few or no tables or charts, and no paragraph headings to guide the reader from one topic to the next. I refer to this formatting style as the *blur technique*. The reader is faced with pages packed full of words running together, almost indistinguishable from one another. This is understandably hard reading, particularly for the financial novice. Nevertheless, you must remember that no matter how difficult the task of digesting the information presented in this manner, you must persevere. Even the poorest of informational presentations in an MD&A offers some clues to a company's financial position. No matter how difficult the task, digging up this information is worth the effort.

Segmentation

Second, and somewhat related to the formatting issue, is that some companies segment their discussion of the results of operations in the MD&A into two distinct reporting periods instead of viewing the three years as a whole. For example, most people find it easier to evaluate a company's performance by looking at one 1989–91 three-year review as a whole as opposed to breaking up the review into two parts, i.e., a comparison of 1989–90 and 1990–91. Fortunately, not too many companies follow this latter approach. I find this kind of narrative disjointed, and with this type of information, it is hard to plot trends.

Lack of Substantive Content

Third, and perhaps the most serious MD&A problem you may encounter, is the content issue. Little valuable insight is provided if a company chooses to simply recite an assortment of historical data without explaining why changes occurred or indicating where the company is headed in the foreseeable future. I have been disappointed and frustrated on numerous occasions by MD&A presentations of this nature. Regardless of the quality of a company's MD&A presentation, however, something still can be gained in accessing information, albeit limited, that does not appear elsewhere in an annual report. If the management commentary lacks insightful perspective, then you must attempt to formulate your own opinions from what information is provided.

□ TURNING HINDSIGHT INTO INSIGHT

As mentioned previously, the MD&A narrative focuses on three principal aspects of a company's financial position: its results of operations, which, in effect, takes a detailed look at the income statement, and the adequacy of capital resources and liquidity to fund operations.

Before I highlight the informational insights that are provided in the MD&A, you should be aware that more in-depth explanations of the evaluative indicators relating to the balance sheet and the statements of income and cash flows will be found in the respective chapters of this book that deal with these subject matters.

Results of Operations

The commentary on the results of operations is the company's analysis of its income and expense performance over the past three years reviewed in its annual report. Hopefully, some clues to future performance also are provided. Look for an explanation of why sales increased, or decreased, which should include, for example, percentage changes due to volume, price, foreign currency fluctuations and acquisitions. Often specifics are provided on the individual performance of products and/or business segments if the company is a multiline operation. General economic and marketplace conditions may be cited as helping or hindering the prospects for a growth in sales.

Other factors affecting revenues and expenses may include comments on distribution systems, product improvements, manufacturing capacity, research and development efforts, tax legislation and nonrecurring income and expense items. Profit margin percentages for gross, operating, pretax and net income generally are given, and variances should be explained. Of particular interest, among other items, is management's view on cost factors, e.g., the stability of raw material costs, interest expense, competition and inflation. In summary, a narrative that provides answers or insights on *why* the numbers changed, and even better, what might be the effects on the company's operational results in the future, is valuable in assessing a company's financial performance.

Capital Resources

With respect to capital resources, the commentary aims to assure the reader that the company is financially strong and is able to adequately fund its operations. In fact, a statement to that effect, in this section, seems to be routine for most companies. Suffice it to say, you must make up your own mind after digesting considerably more information than just relying on an affirmative statement from management. Nevertheless, in addition to the customary affirmation of the company's strong financial condition, you also will find information regarding the company's policy on indebtedness, i.e., how much or how little debt management feels is prudent, what plans it may have for debt financing and a discussion of some relevant debt ratios. Look for ratings on a company's debt from credit agencies such as Moody's, Standard & Poor's, Fitch and Duff & Phelps. Capital expenditures is an obligatory item requiring comment, and information on acquisitions and expansion plans generally is provided. The principal point that management attempts to convey is that cash flows and/or long-term borrowing capacity are adequate to fund the company's growth.

Liquidity

Management's comments on liquidity focus on the company's ability to have sufficient cash available to meet its short-term, i.e., day-to-day, operational obligations. The current ratio, cash flows from operations, turnover ratios for receivables and inventory and the availability of credit facilities, all items that you will learn more about in subsequent chapters, sometimes are presented. Briefly, these are traditional indicators of a company's liquidity and are discussed to demonstrate the adequacy of a company's liquidity position to support its current activities.

As mentioned previously, the information contained in the MD&A section is not audited. In addition, you should not let your expectations for financial insight from the MD&A exceed what most companies actually deliver. These are important points to remember. The MD&A narrative is management's perception of the company's financial position with respect to three important aspects of a company's operations. Despite admonitions by the SEC, corporate practice still tends to reflect more of a historical explanatory approach to the informational content of the MD&A section rather than the prospective slant advocated by the SEC. The latter is obviously much more useful to annual report users. Both preparers and users of management's discussion and analysis information would be better served if the historical performance of a company (hindsight) could be used as a basis to look forward (insight). Nevertheless, the MD&A material contains qualitative observations on a company's financial and investment characteristics that will help you put together a more complete corporate financial profile.

6 OVERVIEW OF THE FINANCIALS

□ THE FINANCIAL STATEMENTS

A publicly held company's audited financial statements, otherwise referred to by the experts as a company's *financials*, must appear in the company's annual report. These statements consist of a balance sheet, a statement of income, a statement of cash flows and a statement of shareholders' equity. While a statement of retained earnings is used infrequently, this statement is presented by some companies, either separately or as an add-on to the income statement, and reflects the changes in this component of shareholders' equity. As will be explained in Chapter 10, the equity and/or retained earnings statements are of little interest or value when analyzing a company's financial position. This chapter, like the professionals, will focus on those financials that track a company's profitability, financial condition and ability to generate cash. This means taking a fundamental look at the statement of income, balance sheet and statement of cash flows, respectively.

John Tracey, author and educator, in his widely read book, *How To Read A Financial Report*, provides a description of the tasks of corporate managers that can be easily reconfigured for you to use as a concise conceptual guide for appraising a company's financial statements:

> The ability of managers to make sales and to control expenses, and thereby to earn profit, is measured in the income statement. Clearly, earning an adequate profit is the key for survival and the manager's most important imperative . . . Managers must also control the financial condition of the business. This means keeping the assets and liabilities within proper limits and proportions relative to each other and relative to the sales and expense levels of the company [the balance sheet]. And, managers must prevent cash shortages that would cause the business to default on its liabilities or to miss a payroll [the cash flow statement].

How well a company handles these management tasks is reflected in its financials. Thus, to adequately judge a company's performance and financial position, you must understand what the financial statements tell you. In the succeeding chapters, I will identify and explain the key elements involved in interpreting and analyzing the balance sheet, the statement of income and the statement of cash flows. Before you get into the specifics, you must understand a number of general characteristics of these statements to help you in your appraisal of a company's financial and investment qualities.

Perspective

The presentation of a company's financial position, as portrayed in its financial statements, is highly influenced in many instances by management estimates and judgments. Financial accounting is not an exact science. In the best of circumstances, management is scrupulously honest and candid; and the outside auditors are demanding, strict and uncompromising. Even in this best-case scenario, the opportunity exists for management to interpret and select a variety of financial accounting decisions. Some companies abuse this latitude. I suspect most do not. Whatever the case, the imprecision inherent in the accounting process means that the prudent student of financial statements should adopt what Leopold Bernstein, a recognized authority on financial analysis, calls "an inquiring and skeptical approach" to financial statements. In an article in *Business Credit* (February 1992), he advises that "analytical safety resides mostly in an attitude of skeptical and informed alertness toward all accounting presentations."

Economic and Industry Conditions

As this book is being written, the U.S. economy is in the second year of what has been considered a rather severe economic recession. Business failures during this period have been high. Many of those companies might well have had decent-looking, if not great-looking financials. But when the economic climate turns bad, a strong financial position and astute management are needed to weather the storm. Conversely, during boom times, when everything is going well, business mistakes and weaknesses are often concealed. When looking at a company's numbers, think of them within the context of what is going on out there in the marketplace.

Martin Fridson in his book, *Financial Statement Analysis*, uses the demise of the Schlitz Brewing Company in 1982 to illustrate how competitive industry forces can undermine an apparently satisfactory financial position. In the case of Schlitz, it was the unintended victim of an intense competitive struggle between Anheuser-Busch and Miller Brewing. As a consequence, Schlitz lost its market share, encountered financial difficulties and eventually was acquired by another competitor. Fridson comments that cases such as Schlitz, among others he discusses in his book, "reinforce the point that analysts of financial statements must not merely examine the numbers, but also strive to understand what underlies them." In other words, economic and industry conditions, favorable or unfavorable, dictate against viewing any company's financial statements in splendid isolation.

Consolidated Statements

Consolidation of a parent company and its majority-owned (more than 50 percent ownership) subsidiaries means that the combined activities of a number of separate legal entities are expressed as one economic unit. The presumption exists that consolidated financial statements are more meaningful than separate statements for all the different entities, which is indicated when the term *consolidated* appears in the title of the financials.

Before 1988, companies could elect not to consolidate dissimilar businesses even though they were majority owned. Insurance, real estate and financing activities were common examples of these businesses. Beginning in 1988, companies then were required to consolidate majority-owned subsidiaries regardless of any dissimilarities in their respective operations: for example, financial services subsidiaries of industrial firms. Thus, today, companies such as General Electric and

Ford now include their respective finance companys' numbers in their consolidated financial statements.

To get an accurate view of companies with consolidated but disparate businesses, the annual report reader needs to segregate or unbundle the consolidated financial information and look at the parts. Otherwise, the standard measurements of financial condition and performance would suffer considerable distortion. Many companies in this circumstance, realizing the complexity of their operations, have adapted their financial statement formats to conform to this reality.

The 50 Percent Solution Be aware that a parent company can limit its ownership to 50 percent, or even less, and still effectively control a subsidiary. This allows the parent to treat this relationship as an equity investment. Under this arrangement, the subsidiary's financial position is not consolidated with that of the parent company. Interestingly enough, these subsidiaries often carry substantial debt that, without the consolidation, is not reflected in the parent's balance sheet. By excluding the high levels of indebtedness of the subsidiary, the parent company's balance sheet looks healthier. Cynics refer to this circumstance as the "50 percent" solution to an otherwise highly leveraged financial position.

Dates

The balance sheet represents a company's financial position at its fiscal year-end, i.e., the last day of its accounting period. In contrast, the income and cash flow statements reflect a company's operations for the full fiscal year. A company's fiscal year is its business year, which does not necessarily correspond to a calendar year. Many companies select periods that end when their business activities have reached the lowest points in their annual cycles. This period is referred to as a *natural* business year. For example, retailing companies generally use January 31st.

Some companies choose a year-end by designating a point in time, e.g., the first Friday in September, which can produce different size fiscal years from one year to another. For a company with a relatively large sales volume, the difference in sales and earnings between a 52-week and a 53-week fiscal year could be significant! This phenomenon must be recognized when comparing such a company's year-to-year results.

In financial reporting, however, even the simple can be made complicated. A good example of this is the following note to the financial statements for a company (name withheld to protect the guilty!) on its fiscal year. Fortunately, we do not see many of these in annual reports:

> Fiscal Year: The Company's fiscal year is the 52 or 53 weeks ending the last Saturday in May. The 52-week years are comprised of 13 four-week accounting periods separated into two 12-week quarters ending during August and November, a 16-week quarter ending during March, and a 12-week quarter ending during May. A 53-week year results in a five-week accounting period and a 13-week quarter at the beginning of the fiscal year.

Statement Nomenclature

The variety of terminology used by companies to describe both their statements and statement account captions can be confusing, especially for a beginner. I cover this inconsistent use of language among companies in each individual chapter on the financials in this book. But I also strongly recommend that you use the glossary at the end of this book to become more familiar with financial statement accounting jargon.

Numbers

The larger the company, the larger the numbers in its financials. In these cases, the numbers generally are rounded off to smaller, more readable digital groupings. This is obviously helpful; however, the presentation of these numbers for their respective fiscal years in most financial statements is not. Let me explain.

Usually, one does not think that a foreign-language proficiency could help improve the reading of financial statements, but it would if that language were Arabic. In its written form, Arabic is read from right to left, requiring the eye to move unnaturally for those of us untrained in Arabic. Nevertheless, this is precisely the chronological order of yearly presentations of financial figures in most financial statements. The purpose is, apparently, to highlight the most recent year.

A few companies, if only others would follow their example, present their numbers in the other direction, from left to right, just the way the eye moves naturally. I think it is easier for most people to track the progression of events and detect changes with this type of format, and I have used this technique in my illustrations in the following chapters. After all, there must be some significance to the inclusion of *logical* in the composition of the word chronological! A conspiracy may inadvertently have been discovered here: Have you noticed that the numbers on a calculator are upside down from those on a push-button telephone?

One last item on numbers. When comparing an amount in the statement of income (e.g., net income) or the statement of cash flows (e.g., operating cash flows) to a balance sheet amount (e.g., total assets), it is more accurate to use an average for the balance sheet amount when calculating indicators and ratios. Sometimes this is done for you in annual report presentations of financial information; other times it is not. Averaging simply involves taking the appropriate year-end figures, adding them together and dividing the total by two. This is a rough but useful approximation of a representative balance sheet amount for the whole year, as opposed to just using the amount for the last day of the year. Remember, the income and cash flow financial figures represent *flow numbers*, and the balance sheet figures represent *point-in-time numbers*.

Notes to Financial Statements

This component of an annual report presentation is of such importance that it requires a detailed discussion in Chapter 12. Suffice it to say here that the notation on each financial statement making reference to the notes should be taken very seriously. These notes are as important as the financials themselves. The information in these notes is critical to a full understanding of the numbers in a company's balance sheet, statement of income and statement of cash flows.

All the literature on financial statement analysis universally attests to the importance of and the need to read the accompanying notes. And yet, it is common annual report practice to print these notations on the financials in microscopic size, which requires the use of a magnifying glass to read these notes, at least for some of us with less than perfect vision. Adding insult to injury, the phraseology often is equally as weak, as in the use of the anemic admonition, "See accompanying notes." What is needed here is to send a powerful, motivating message of "industrial strength" to the reader, e.g., THE ACCOMPANYING NOTES ARE AN INTEGRAL PART OF THESE FINANCIAL STATEMENTS. A few companies do this, but many do not. Therefore, always keep this message in mind, regardless of how it is expressed in a company's financial statements.

Financial Ratios

A ratio takes absolute numbers from a company's financial statements and converts them into meaningful relationships and indicators. Financial ratios are expressed either as a times multiple (×) or as a percentage (%). Looked at over an extended period of time and/or compared to other companies and industry averages, they provide insight into a company's financial condition and performance. A list of possible ratios and indicators would be extremely long. Generally, they are grouped into five broad categories: liquidity, debt, profitability, cash flow and market measures. I will use and explain a number of these ratios as I review the specific financial statements in the following chapters.

Remember, however, that ratios have their limitations. They are not meant to be absolute answers but rather clues to further understanding. Depending on the industry and on a company's stage of development, a good ratio for one business might not be appropriate for another. Also, as I mentioned previously, ratios become meaningful only when tracked over time to reflect trends.

In an annual report, ratios usually are employed in the financial highlights, historical summary of financial data and management discussion and analysis sections. Unfortunately, the reader is confronted with a lack of standardization as to what ratios are used and, most important, how they are computed. Only occasionally are explanations provided regarding what components are used to calculate the ratios. In view of this lack of precision, I recommend that you fully understand how the financial ratios you find in an annual report are computed before accepting their meaning at face value. Exhibit 6.1 identifies and explains those financial ratios that tend to appear most frequently in annual reports. These ratios and other indicators will be discussed in detail in succeeding chapters.

A word of caution on using industry averages as a comparative tool. In today's business environment, a company often is a hybrid, operating in several lines of business. Differing accounting policies among companies also can make comparisons a bit tricky. Finally, if you use ratio information services, be sure to recognize any differences in their computation methods. For these reasons, industry averages also have their limitations.

Additional Ratio Information In any case, for those readers interested in becoming familiar with industry ratio information, three of the more well-known services are:

- Dun & Bradstreet, Inc., *Key Business Ratios*, 99 Church Street, New York, NY 10007
- Robert Morris Associates, *Annual Statement Studies*, PNB Building, Philadelphia, PA 19107
- Leo Troy's *Almanac of Business & Industrial Financial Ratios*, Prentice Hall, Business & Professional Division, Englewood Cliffs, NJ 07632

Multiyear Comparisons

The SEC requires annual report presentations to include three years of audited income, cash flow and equity financial statements but only two years for the balance sheet. Most companies follow this practice. Those companies that deviate from this approach and provide three years of their balance sheets are to be praised. The calculation of averages and a number of balance sheet dependent ratios are greatly facilitated by having three-year balance sheet data readily available. Also, as you will recall from my remarks concerning statement presentations in the financial highlights section, a two-year comparison is simply not meaningful.

Five years of financial data provides a reasonable basis for judging a company's historical performance and for detecting trends in key indicators. Three years are a bare minimum. However, just undertaking a minimal three-year financial statement analysis requires four years of financials (for a base year and to calculate three-year averages), which means that the information in one annual report will not suffice. Also, because most companies provide only two years of balance sheets in their annual reports, your efforts are further complicated.

For example, 1991 and 1990 annual reports will give you only three years of balance sheets—1991, 1990 and 1989. You can solve this problem by obtaining two annual reports, two years apart. The 1991 and 1989 annual reports will have balance sheets for 1991–90 and 1989–88, respectively. The nuance of the use of the plural form of annual report in this book's title now should be evident!

In the chapters on the balance sheet and income statements, you will be shown how to construct simple multiyear spreadsheets to help you analyze these financials. Several computer spreadsheet programs can help you do this, but you also can do your analysis with a little more time and effort, paper, pencil and the smallest, most basic calculator. If you are not computer-literate, do not be deterred from crunching the numbers by hand. Manual number-crunching is a good way for the novice to get a feel for what the numbers mean and how they can be used to evaluate a company's financial position.

Statements

You should be aware that a company is permitted to use two sets of books for its accounting records. It can apply different accounting methods to the financials used for its tax return as opposed to the financials prepared for its public financial reporting. The expressions *tax reporting purposes* refers to the former and *financial statement purposes* to the latter. For tax purposes, companies employ accounting policies to defer tax payments by reporting lower pretax income. On the other hand, companies want to maximize reported earnings to enhance the presentation of their financial statements for investors, creditors and the general public.

This completes the overview of the general characteristics of a company's financial statements as they appear in an annual report. In the next four chapters, I will guide you through a focused look at what you need to know about each individual statement. Financial statement analysis is a vast and somewhat complex subject. It has been written about extensively over the years. Because of space limitations, I have purposely been selective in the points I think need to be covered. At the risk of oversimplifying, I would prefer to convey a few fundamental insights, which can be easily applied, as opposed to confusing you with a mass of sophisticated analytical techniques. The latter approach goes beyond the scope of this book. My concluding remarks in Chapter 17 contain recommended sources for you to use to broaden your financial and investment analysis skills beyond the fundamentals provided here.

The financial statements of the fictional ABC Corporation, otherwise referred to as ABC Corp., are found in Exhibits 7.2, 9.1, 10.1 and 11.1. These statements come from a real-life company and are fairly representative in their content and format. Exceptions are duly noted. The figures are used to illustrate conceptual points, calculate ratios and explain financial indicators contained in the text of Chapters 7 to 11.

EXHIBIT 6.1 Typical Annual Report Financial Ratios

RATIOS	METHOD(S) OF COMPUTATION[1]	WHAT THEY MEAN
Liqudity:		
CURRENT RATIO (×)	$$\frac{\text{Current Assets}}{\text{Current Liabilities}}$$	A basic test of short-term liquidity.
QUICK ASSETS RATIO (×)	$$\frac{\text{Cash and Cash Equivalents} + \text{Marketable Securities} + \text{Accounts Receivable}}{\text{Current Liabilities}}$$ or $$\frac{\text{Current Assets} - \text{Inventory}}{\text{Current Liabilities}}$$	The focus here is on those current assets that can be readily converted to cash to pay current obligations. The higher the ratio, the lower the dependence on selling inventory to pay current liabilities.
DAYS' SALES OUTSTANDING (DSO)	a. $$\frac{\text{Net Sales}}{365 \text{ Days}} = \text{Sales per Day}$$ b. $$\frac{\text{Average Accounts Receivable}^{[2]}}{\text{Sales per Day}} = \text{DSO}$$	Indicates how many days it is taking to convert uncollected sales to cash. A short turnover period and a stable or declining trend are positive indicators of receivable quality.
DAYS' SALES IN INVENTORY OR INVENTORY TURNOVER	a. $$\frac{\text{Cost of Sales}}{365 \text{ Days}} = \text{Sales per Day}$$ b. $$\frac{\text{Average Inventory}}{\text{Sales per Day}} = \text{Days' Sales in Inventory}^{[3]}$$	A rough guide as to the number of days it takes to sell the company's inventory—how quickly it is moving. The shorter the turnover period, the greater the quality and liquidity of inventories.

1. An inconsistency in terminology and methods of computation makes it difficult to be completely accurate in these descriptions of ratio computations.

2. To be technically correct, the gross trade accounts receivable amount, i.e., net trade receivables plus the allowance for doubtful accounts, should be used.

3. This ratio is most often expressed in annual reports as a times multiple, e.g., 60 days sales in inventory represents, approximately, a turnover rate of six times.

EXHIBIT 6.1 Typical Annual Report Financial Ratios (continued)

RATIOS	METHOD(S) OF COMPUTATION[1]	WHAT THEY MEAN
Debt or Leverage:		
DEBT RATIO (%)	$$\frac{\text{Total Liabilities}}{\text{Total Assets}}$$	Indicates the percentage of assets financed by liabilities as opposed to equity, i.e., the degree of financial leverage.
DEBT/EQUITY OR DEBT TO WORTH RATIO (%)	$$\frac{\text{Total Liabilities}}{\text{Shareholders' Equity}}$$ or $$\frac{\text{Debt Obligations}^{[2]}}{\text{Shareholders' Equity}}$$	Measures how much the creditors/lenders have put into the company versus the shareholders. The lower the percentage, the greater the company's financial safety and operating freedom.
CAPITALIZATION RATIO (%)	$$\frac{\text{Long-Term Debt}}{\text{Long-Term Debt + Shareholders' Equity}}$$	Indicates the makeup of a company's permanent capital (capitalization) — what is provided by debt as opposed to the shareholders' investment. The lower the percentage, the smaller the debt and the larger the equity.
INTEREST COVERAGE RATIO (X)	$$\frac{\text{Pretax Income + Interest Expense}^{[3]}}{\text{Interest Expense}}$$	Indicates how many times interest expense could increase before a company's ability to meet interest payments would be questioned. The higher the ratio, the greater the servicing capacity.

1. An inconsistency in terminology and methods of computation makes it difficult to be completely accurate in these descriptions of ratio computations.

2. There is considerable latitude evidenced in what is considered debt. It ranges from being synonymous with total liabilities to very narrow definitions of debt.

3. Some analysts would consider also adding one-third of the operating lease rental costs to the interest expense.

EXHIBIT 6.1 Typical Annual Report Financial Ratios (continued)

RATIOS	METHOD(S) OF COMPUTATION[1]	WHAT THEY MEAN
Profitability:		
RETURN ON ASSETS (ROA) RATIO (%)	$$\frac{\text{Net Income}^{[2]}}{\text{Average Total Assets}}$$	Measures the profitability of a company's total resources. The higher the return, the more effective utilization of assets.
RETURN ON EQUITY (ROE) RATIO (%)	$$\frac{\text{Net Income}^{[2]}}{\text{Average Shareholders' Equity}}$$	Measures the profits being generated on the shareholders' invested capital. The higher the ratio, the greater the yield.
RETURN ON INVESTED CAPITAL OR CAPITAL EMPLOYED RATIO (%)	$$\frac{\text{Net Income}^{[2]}}{\text{Average: Shareholders' Equity + Long-Term Debt}}$$	This indicator expands on the ROE ratio to include borrowed funds along with shareholders' equity.
RETURN ON SALES RATIO (%)	$$\frac{\text{Net Income}^{[2]}}{\text{Net Sales}}$$	Reveals the profitablity of sales. The higher return a company is able to generate from its sales, the more efficient its operations.

1. An inconsistency in terminology and methods of computation makes it difficult to be completely accurate in these descriptions of ratio computations.

2. Sometimes operating income or pretax income are used as the numerator.

7

THE BALANCE SHEET

☐ WHAT A COMPANY OWNS AND OWES

The subject matter of this chapter and the next, the balance sheet, is an important financial statement that records, as of a company's fiscal year-end, the company's assets (resources of value that it owns), liabilities (obligations to others) and shareholders' equity (the owners' investment). As mentioned previously, the balance sheet is a photograph at a specific point in time of a company's financial position as reflected in the fundamental accounting equation:

$$\text{Assets} = \text{Liabilities} + \text{Equity}$$

The importance of this seemingly simple relationship will be explained later. First, however, several structural considerations that should help you better understand the balance sheet as a source of investment and financial information will be discussed.

Balance Sheet Formats

Standard accounting conventions generally present the balance sheet in one of two formats: the account form (horizontal) or the report form (vertical). Another format, the financial position form, is used infrequently in the United States but is quite commonly used internationally, particularly by European companies. Examples of these three forms are illustrated in Exhibit 7.1, along with representative account titles that make up the major balance sheet components. The numbers used in these condensed statements are the same as those found in the fictitious ABC Corporation's balance sheet portrayed in Exhibit 7.2, which is fairly typical in terms of its structure and content. We will refer to the ABC statement to illustrate various points as we discuss the balance sheet in this chapter and the next.

The account and report formats for the balance sheet are fairly standardized into sections for assets, liabilities and equity. These sections are further divided into subsections, which sometimes include current (short-term) and noncurrent (long-term) classifications. Curious as it may seem, the word noncurrent most often is used to describe *long-term* assets; and the word *long-term* is employed generally to describe *noncurrent* liabilities. Do not be confused, for the terms *noncurrent* and *long-term* in financial accounting terminology are synonymous.

Generally, assets are listed in the descending order of their liquidity and liabilities, similarly, in the order of their priority for payment. This is an important point and dictates the nature of this review of the balance sheet. This chapter will focus on what is important about a company's current or working capital position. In Chapter 8, I will review the permanent capital position, i.e., fixed assets, long-term debt and equity accounts. But first, let us look at the forest before getting to the trees.

□ ASSETS = LIABILITIES + EQUITY

As mentioned previously, the so-called balance sheet equation of assets = liabilities + equity describes what a balance sheet represents. An important analytical perspective, however, is hidden in this deceptively simple formula. You do not have to be a sophisticated financial analyst to understand what the equation very clearly indicates: As the assets of a company grow, its liabilities and/or equity also must grow for things to stay in balance.

What is so important about this rather obvious relationship? A company grows, or gets bigger, by increasing sales and/or by acquiring other businesses. In both cases, this more than likely results in higher levels of receivables and inventory and requires a greater investment in property, plant and equipment (fixed assets) to support the growth or expansion. The previously mentioned balance sheet accounts are, as can be seen in the ABC Corporation's balance sheet, usually a

EXHIBIT 7.1 Balance Sheet Formats and Representative Account Structure

ACCOUNT FORM

Current assets	$262,006	Current liabilities	$ 76,763
Fixed assets	59,929	Long-term liabilities	54,126
Other assets	2,240	Shareholders' equity	193,286
Total assets	$324,175	Total liabilities/equity	$324,175

REPORT FORM

Current assets	$262,006
Fixed assets	59,929
Other assets	2,240
Total assets	$324,175
Current liabilities	$ 76,763
Long-term liabilities	54,126
Shareholders' equity	193,286
Total liabilities/equity	$324,175

FINANCIAL POSITION FORM

Current assets	$262,006
Less: current liabilities	−76,763
Working Capital	185,243
Plus: noncurrent assets	62,169
Total assets less current liabilities	247,412
Less: long-term liabilities	54,126
Net assets	$193,286

REPRESENTATIVE ACCOUNT STRUCTURE

Current assets:
Cash, cash equivalents, marketable securities, accounts receivable, inventories, prepaid expenses and other current assets.

Noncurrent assets:
Investments; property, plant and equipment (commonly referred to as fixed assets), intangible assets and other assets.

Current liabilities:
Notes payable or short-term borrowings, accounts payable, accrued expenses and liabilities, income tax payable and current portion of long-term debt.

Long-term liabilities:
Long-term debt, deferred taxes and other long-term obligations.

Shareholders' equity:
Preferred stock, common stock, additional paid-in capital, retained earnings and possibly these adjustment accounts: treasury stock, foreign currency translation and guaranteed ESOP obligation.

EXHIBIT 7.2 Consolidated Balance Sheets—The ABC Corporation

Years ended December 31 (in thousands, except per-share amounts)	1991	1990
ASSETS **CURRENTS ASSETS:**		
Cash and cash equivalents	$ 92,252	$ 18,482
Accounts receivable, net of allowance for doubtful accounts of $5,749 in 1991, $3,567 in 1990	72,335	64,768
Inventories	73,451	91,639
Prepaid expenses	18,036	20,416
Other current assets	5,932	4,681
Total current assets	262,006	199,986
Plant, property and equipment	83,236	63,729
Accumulated depreciation and amortization	(23,307)	(17,077)
Net plant, property and equipment	59,929	46,652
Excess of cost over net assets acquired	2,240	3,703
Other assets	–	10,778
Total assets	$324,175	$261,119
LIABILITIES AND SHAREHOLDERS' EQUITY **CURRENT LIABILITIES:**		
Short-term borrowings	$ 704	$ –
Accounts payable	29,304	32,806
Accrued salaries, wages and employee benefits	10,240	5,424
Other accrued liabilities	27,382	14,554
Income taxes payable	8,397	4,715
Current portion of long-term debt	736	713
Total current liabilities	76,763	58,212
Long-term debt	30,126	81,045
Deferred income taxes	24,000	13,063
Commitments and contingencies		
SHAREHOLDERS' EQUITY:		
Common stock, par value $.01; 30,000,000 shares authorized; 15,254,695 shares issues and outstanding in 1991; 11,628,334 in 1990	153	117
Additional paid-in capital	83,917	34,533
Retained earnings	109,216	74,149
Total shareholders' equity	193,286	108,799
Total liabilities & shareholders' equity	$324,175	$261,119

The accompanying notes are an integral part of the financial statements.

company's principal assets. In the case of ABC, an unusually large, temporary cash balance was on hand at the end of 1991.

As a generalization, these accounts—receivables, inventory and fixed assets—will typically reflect the *big numbers* in most companies' asset positions in their balance sheets. These numbers will be discussed in more detail later on, but for now, it is important to realize that growth generally dictates a larger asset base, which, in turn, requires a larger *right side* of the equation—more liabilities and/or equity. Within this phenomenon lies important clues to a company's financial and investment qualities.

How assets are supported, or financed, by a corresponding growth in liabilities and equity reveals a lot about a company's financial health, particularly in the case of a growth-oriented company. According to a basic rule of finance, short-term and long-term (noncurrent) assets should be financed by sources of funds with the same characteristics on the liability/equity side. A reasonable mix of short- and long-term debt liabilities and proportionately appropriate levels of long-term debt and equity are the signs of a financially healthy company. No absolutely right mix or proportion is applicable to every company. Different industries, as well as the various stages of development in a company's life, will reflect a diversity of positions. However, taking a conservative stance and learning from the borrowing excesses of companies in the 1980s, it is essential for you to look at balance sheets with a critical eye when you are appraising how assets are supported.

Rapid "Growth" Out of Business

A rapid growth in sales and assets often is viewed as a positive corporate attribute. This can be the case, but not always, depending on how the growth in sales and assets is financed. If a proper mix of short-term and long-term sources of funding, both debt and equity, are not carefully orchestrated, a company can actually *grow* out of business. At the very least it can encounter difficulties in operating profitably. Let us take a look at how the dynamics of the balance sheet equation are reflected in the following, admittedly simplistic, illustrations for the fictional Zoom Corporation. If you need to refresh your memory on the ratios mentioned here, refer back to Exhibit 6.1 on page 35 in Chapter 6. The abbreviations used in the illustrated balance sheets are explained as follows:

CA	= current assets
NCA	= noncurrent assets
A	= total assets
CL	= current liabilities
LTD	= long-term debt
SE	= shareholders' equity
L&SE	= total liabilities and shareholders' equity.

Beginning in year one, things look pretty good (see Exhibit 7.3). Zoom Corporation ends the year with a solid current ratio, evidences a conservative low-debt position and has a very strong equity base. The trade creditors and lenders love Zoom.

In year two, the sales of "Zoomies" really take off, and a consequent increase in receivables and inventories supports these sales (see Exhibit 7.4). The increase in current assets is therefore significant, accompanied by a big increase in fixed assets. Zoom management bets on even bigger sales growth in the future and invests heavily in machinery and equipment to support this process. Profits are good but nowhere near sufficient to fund the new level of operations. So Zoom uses its supplier credit and taps all its short-term credit lines with banks. A small long-term loan is arranged, but it is easier to access short-term credit facilities. However, Zoom's current position deteriorates dramatically from the previous year. Also, with assets doubling in size and equity increasing by only 15 percent, the company becomes debt-heavy from one year to the next.

EXHIBIT 7.3 Zoom Corporation Year One Balance Sheet

					Ratios	
CA	$200	CL	$ 50		Current	4.0:1
		LTD	$ 50			
					Debt	33%
NCA	$100	SE	$200		Capitalization	20%
Total A	$300	Total L&SE	$300			

EXHIBIT 7.4 Zoom Corporation Year Two Balance Sheet

						Ratios
CA	$300	CL	$270	Current		1.1:1
NCA	$300	LTD	$100	Debt		62%
		SE	$230			
				Capitalization		30%
Total A	$600	Total L&SE	$600			

Year three was a poor year for profits (see Exhibit 7.5). Costs went up significantly, particularly interest expense. "Zoomie" sales still were strong, so management continued expanding the physical plant to increase production capacity. Unwilling, or more likely unable, to raise equity capital, Zoom was successful in arranging a long-term loan. However, Zoom now is highly leveraged, with a tight current position. The debt and capitalization ratios are at worrisome levels and management is spending a lot of time on finance matters. Zoom Corporation has enjoyed a dramatic increase in sales and tripled in asset size. And now it is in big trouble! Unless Zoom can restructure

EXHIBIT 7.5 Zoom Corporation Year Three Balance Sheet

						Ratios
CA	$350	CL	$300	Current		1.2:1
		LTD	$420	Debt		76%
NCA	$600	SE	$230	Capitalization		68%
Total A	$950	Total L&SE	$950			

the liability/equity side of its balance sheet, the risks of *growing* out of business are substantial.

While this example is a bit contrived and simplistic, it is intended to make the point that asset growth, unless it is properly managed and financed, actually can jeopardize the future of a company. The balance sheet equation, besides being descriptive, serves as a simple reminder of this important consideration. It is time now to examine more closely some of the key components in the current position of the balance sheet that provide indicators of a company's financial well-being.

☐ EXAMINING THE BALANCE SHEET'S CURRENT POSITION

The current position of a balance sheet is reflected in the relationship between current assets and current liabilities. Actually, a number of relationships exist; and I will look at these to determine which are the most important for you to understand and why. But first, let us review ABC Corporation's balance sheet in Exhibit 7.2 to make sure that we understand what these current assets and liabilities represent.

Except for the absence of an entry for marketable securities, ABC Corporation's current assets are fairly representative of this category of assets. It is worthwhile noting that ABC Corporation's accounts receivable represent trade accounts with nontrade items such as insurance claims and tax refunds being accounted for in other current assets. Some companies use the caption *trade receivables* or *accounts receivable—trade* to make this distinction. This consideration may not always be that relevant, but financial professionals prefer to use trade receivables as the component for the calculation of the quick assets and the receivable turnover ratios, which are discussed later in this chapter. You will see that the inclusion of nontrade items, if material, would tend to distort the intent of these measurements. Regarding ABC Corporation's current liabilities, here again, there is nothing unusual in its balance sheet presentation. Some companies might aggregate all their *accruals*, or actually use that term, in one account for the various expenses pending payment as of the statement date. Contrary to the practice with receivables, a company's accounts payable generally are assumed to represent obligations to vendors and trade suppliers as opposed to expense accruals. Sometimes accounts payable and accrued expenses are lumped together in one account.

Theoretically, current liabilities should be paid off from the cash and conversion to cash of current assets. The sequence of events is easy to follow:

1. A company acquires goods and services.

2. These are processed and/or stored as inventory.

3. As goods are sold from inventory, receivables are created for sales to customers on credit terms (retailers and food-service businesses have cash sales).

4. As receivables are collected and cash accumulated, bank borrowings, vendors and suppliers and other current obligations are paid when due.

In simple terms, this process constitutes a company's operating cycle, which is repeated over and over during a company's business year. Before discussing the importance of this phenomenon, you must first become familiar with two commonly used measurements of a company's current position.

□ A NEW LOOK AT SOME OLD GUIDELINES

The Current Ratio

The *current ratio,* which compares current assets to current liabilities, appears frequently and prominently in annual reports. As a basic test of a company's short-term liquidity, the current ratio is important to creditors, particularly banks and suppliers, as well as investors. Its simplicity and ease of calculation have made its reporting widespread. Conventional wisdom assumes that the higher the ratio, the more capacity there is to pay current liabilities. In addition, almost all the literature on financial statement analysis, at least that directed at the less experienced beginner, will pay homage to a 2-to-1 current ratio or higher as a desirable standard.

The ABC Corporation's 1991 current ratio is 3.4 to 1 ($262,006 ÷ $76,763 = 3.4$x$). While recognizing that more of a good thing is better, the truth of the matter is that there are any number of *desirable* current ratios. What is desirable depends on the industry and the nature of a company's business. Also, committed bank credit lines and shelf registrations for debt and equity securities enhance a company's current position, but these facilities are not reflected in the balance sheet. The diversity of circumstances evident in this universe of possibilities should make it clear that it is virtually impossible to suggest any one numerical relationship is more desirable than another.

To help you understand this point with a real-life example, I recommend that you obtain a copy of Pepsico's 1991 annual report. You will see that its 1990 balance sheet shows current liabilities exceeding its current assets (also true for 1989). Was something wrong there? Not to worry. Pepsico is considered a well-run, financially strong company. The management analysis remarks in its annual reports habitually emphasize the cash nature of its business and appropriately highlight its negative working capital position as an *interest-free source of capital*. You will learn to appreciate this position more when I discuss the operating cycle later in this chapter. Suffice it to say for now that Pepsico is referring to the fact that it is tying up a relatively small amount of cash to support its receivables and inventory, which frees up cash to use for other corporate purposes.

Limitations of the Current Ratio

Continuing with what some commentators might consider analytical heresy, it also is true that, as an indicator of liquidity, the current ratio has several serious limitations. Only when you analyze the cash conversion of receivables and inventories can you get an accurate reading of the liquidity of a company's current position. We will do this with ABC Corporation when we look at working capital and the operating cycle in the next sections of this chapter. This aspect of a company's current position has been understood by financial professionals for many years, but somehow this perspective has not been given the emphasis it deserves when it comes to informing the general public.

Quick Assets Ratio

One more observation should be made on the liquidity issue. While not always accompanying the current ratio in annual report presentations, the quick assets ratio appears on occasion. It further refines the current ratio in this regard. By comparing cash, cash equivalents, marketable securities and receivables (quick assets) to total current liabilities, the quick assets ratio helps determine the liquidity of a company's current assets. The focus here is on those current assets that can be most readily converted to cash to pay current obligations. By excluding inventory, the ratio also is used as an indicator of a company's dependence, or lack of dependence, on inventory to meet these obligations. For example, ABC Corporation's quick assets ratio (1991) of 2.1 to 1 ($92,252 + $72,335 = $164,587 ÷ $76,763 = 2.1$x$) appears to indicate a relatively liquid position, i.e., a low dependence on less liquid inventory assets to meet current liabilities.

The current and quick asset ratios are useful, but you really need to go beyond these somewhat simplistic measurements to obtain a more meaningful view of a company's true current position. Because the current ratio, and to a lesser degree the quick assets ratio, are so widely used in financial reporting, it would be unwise to totally ignore their informational value, albeit limited. A prudent approach would be to use these ratios as a starting point for further analysis. This leads to the next step in determining the strengths and weaknesses of a company's current position—understanding working capital and the operating cycle.

☐ IS WORKING CAPITAL IRRELEVANT?

Yes and no. The answer to this question depends on how you view working capital. Simply defined, working capital is the difference between current assets and current liabilities. In ABC Corporation's case, this would equal $185,243,000 in 1991 ($262,006 − $76,763 = $185,243). As an absolute amount, the manner in which it most often appears in an annual report, it has little or no relevance. To have any meaning, a working capital amount must be compared to something, generally sales or total assets. In addition, the behavior of the components of working capital, particularly as providers and users of cash, is critical to a company's liquidity position. Unfortunately, few annual report presentations provide the depth of information needed to adequately analyze working capital.

If a working capital ratio appears in an annual report, it generally is expressed as a comparison of average working capital to net sales. A high ratio shows *overtrading*, i.e., operating at a very high level of sales with a relatively small amount of working capital. A low ratio may reflect an underutilization of assets. Dividing 1991 ABC net sales of $533,814,000 by average working capital of $163,508,500 results in a working ratio of 3.2*x*.

1991 ABC Corporation net sales: $533,814,000

Average working capital:
$$\frac{[1990] \ \$141,774 + [1991] \ \$185,243}{2} = \frac{\$327,017}{2} = \$163,508$$

Working ratio:

$$\frac{\$533,814,000 \text{ [Net Sales]}}{\$163,508,500 \text{ [Average working capital]}} = 3.2x$$

As you know, to be meaningful, the trend of this ratio would have to be plotted over an extended period of time and some industry comparisons would have to be made.

I have indicated previously that the discussion of working capital is somewhat lacking in most annual report presentations. The working capital numbers generally are displayed and/or mentioned in the financial highlights, the letter to the shareholders, the MD&A section and the historical summary of financial data. However, other than confirming its existence and implying that the amount is adequate, its treatment is cursory. This is unfortunate and requires you to do some serious number-crunching to determine a company's operating cycle, which is the most effective way to analyze a company's current position.

Before we discuss the operating cycle, you need to know that working capital and cash flow are not synonymous. This is an important point. The flow of working capital current assets into cash will not necessarily match the future cash flow needs of the company. In the example of the Zoom Corporation, as a company's sales grow, trade receivables and inventories also grow to accommodate this expansion of its activities. If the growth of these current assets are not contained and/or their turnover rates accelerated, working capital will grow in size and appear satisfactory; but the slow conversion of these assets to cash eventually will squeeze a company's liquidity. Simply stated, you cannot pay bills with working capital; you pay bills with cash!

Even with the proper management of receivables and inventory, a growing company will need more funds to support reasonable levels of these working capital components to keep pace with sales growth. These funds have to come from increased current liabilities (generally bank borrowings and accounts payable), long-term debt or equity. Current liabilities generally cannot grow so fast as current assets, and debt and equity sources may not always be available. This circumstance explains why growth companies do not pay dividends, preferring to *plow back* earnings into the business to meet working capital needs. If sales grow faster than profits and/or the working capital components of the current position evidence a decline in their turnover rates, a company can find itself with a cash problem.

□ THE OPERATING CYCLE

What is the operating cycle? It is an approximation of the time it takes to convert receivables and inventory into cash. This time span can be measured by using the turnover ratios for receivables as expressed as the number of days sales outstanding and the number of days sales in inventory, respectively. Their appearance in annual reports is infrequent. You should note that the concept of turnover can be expressed as a number of times per year or as a number of days. For example, a turnover rate of six times a year, usually expressed as 6*x*, is the same as, approximately, 61 days, and vice versa. When receivable and inventory turnover data is provided in an annual report, it seems customary to use days for receivables and a times multiple for inventory. You can easily convert the latter into days by dividing 365 days by the times multiple (365 ÷ 6 = 61). This exercise is useful for calculating the operating cycle, which is expressed in days.

A fast turnover rate of receivables and inventory creates liquidity and is a positive indication of the quality of these assets, efficient management, profitability and healthy working capital. The longer the collection period for receivables and the slower the movement of inventory, the more cash is needed to carry these current assets. Conversely, the shorter the periods, the less cash is needed. A downward trend (more days outstanding) in the turnover rate for receivables may indicate collection problems or more generous payment terms because of competitive pressures. An upward trend (fewer days outstanding) may mean more efficient collection efforts, better industry conditions or stricter credit terms. Changes in the inventory turnover rate may indicate the positive or negative impacts of raw material sourcing, production, quality and competitive considerations. In brief, a shorter operating cycle translates into a more liquid current position. This provides a company with the ability and flexibility to respond quickly to opportunities and unexpected events. It also means that borrowing requirements and interest expense are less. A trend toward a longer operating cycle reverses all these positive attributes.

Because comprehensive operating cycle information is relatively scarce in most annual reports, you should be equipped to put together the calculations on your own. The numbers used to compute the turnover ratios are easily found in the balance sheet and the income statement. You should be aware of a technical consideration that applies to the inventory ratio. The cost of sales amount is used rather than the net sales amount because profit already is included in net sales. Both the cost of sales and inventory are recorded at cost and, therefore, are more comparable. The net sales and cost of sales figures are found in the income statement.

Following the formulas described in Exhibit 6.1 for days sales in receivables and inventory, let us compute the operating cycle for the ABC Corporation using its 1991 balance sheet (see Exhibit 7.2 on page 44) and its income statement (see Exhibit 9.1 on page 76):

Day sales outstanding:

1. $\dfrac{\$553,814}{365} = \$1,517$ sales per day

2.

1990	1991
$64,768	$72,335
3,567	5,749
$68,335 +	$78,084 = $146,419 ÷ 2 = $73,210 average receivables

3. $\dfrac{\$73,210}{\$1,517} = 48$ days sales outstanding $(365 ÷ 48 = 7.6x)$

Day sales in inventory:

1. $\dfrac{\$360,439}{365} = \$988$ sales per day

2.

1990	1991
$91,639 +	$73,451 = $165,090 ÷ 2 = $82,545 average inventory

3. $\dfrac{\$82,545}{\$988} = 83.5$ days sales in inventory $(365 ÷ 83.5 = 4.3x)$

Based on these calculations, ABC has an operating cycle of 131.5 days (48 + 83.5 = 131.5). Industry comparisons and trends in the operating cycle's aggregate number of days, as well as the individual behavior of its components, tell much more about a company's current position, particularly its liquidity, than a working capital number.

The current, quick assets and working capital ratios are useful, but the operating cycle will tell how fast, or slow, key operating working capital assets are converting to cash. As a cross-check on this concept, it is worth looking at Pepsico's purported highly liquid current position. According to its 1991 annual report figures, its operating cycle registers 53 days (28.7 days sales outstanding and 24.3 days sales in inventory). Even without the benefit of the comparative analysis equivalent of a "taste test" with Coca-Cola (comparing the numbers of two companies in the same industry) or a trend analysis, the indicators appear to confirm Pepsico's extraordinary liquidity. This circumstance permits the company to operate with current ratios and working capital that defy conventional standards.

It should be apparent that an operating cycle analysis is much more meaningful than the traditional guidelines presented in most annual reports. The good news is that all the data you need to perform this type of analysis is in the document. In the following chapter, I will continue to analyze the balance sheet by looking at the long-term or noncurrent structure of assets, liabilities and equity.

8

MORE BALANCE SHEET

☐ THE LONG-TERM POSITION

Having completed the review of the various aspects of the balance sheet's current position, we now will become familiar with the more permanent or long-term components of the balance sheet. Noncurrent assets, long-term liabilities and shareholders' equity, or just plain equity, and some special items will be explained and scrutinized for their significance in understanding a company's financial position. I will continue to use the ABC Corporation's balance sheet appearing in Exhibit 7.2 on page 44 to illustrate various points touched on in this chapter. Finally, Exhibits 8.1, 8.2 and the accompanying text will show you how to use a spreadsheet to improve your understanding of the numbers in a balance sheet.

☐ NONCURRENT ASSETS

Generally, the principal accounts of interest in a company's long-term or noncurrent asset position include its fixed assets, formally identified as property, plant and equipment, and its intangible assets. As you will see, the latter can include a number of items, some more important than others, e.g., purchased goodwill will be looked at closely. First, however, let us dispense with what usually are less significant items sometimes appearing as noncurrent assets.

Unconsolidated Subsidiaries and Affiliates

Investments in unconsolidated subsidiaries and affiliates, i.e., those in which the investor company has less than a 50 percent ownership interest, appear in the balance sheet as noncurrent assets. For that category of investment in the 20 percent to 50 percent range, the investment most likely will be valued on an equity method basis as opposed to those under 20 percent, which are valued at cost. As time goes by, the cost method will not accurately reflect the fortunes, good and bad, of the investee company. Thus, it would be difficult to determine the true asset value of an investor company's minority, unconsolidated investments. The other assets account is oftentimes a *catchall* account. Often deferred charges and other intangible assets are *buried* in this category. If the amount is significant, it bears looking into; otherwise, the account does not warrant much analytical attention.

Property, Plant and Equipment (PP&E)

The property, plant and equipment (PP&E) account represents those assets of a permanent nature that are required to operate the business. Most manufacturing companies require a relatively large investment in fixed assets. Conversely, service companies, wholesalers and distributors require much less in the way of fixed investment. Items such as land, buildings, plant facilities, machinery, equipment, furniture and fixtures, construction in progress, capital lease equipment and leasehold improvements all are considered fixed investments. Among other considerations, the issue of value is probably the most important item in any discussion of a balance sheet's fixed asset amount.

The concept of depreciating fixed assets is fairly easy to understand. With the exception of land, which is not depreciated, the different types of fixed assets are depreciated according to their estimated useful lives. Annual reports do not provide much detailed information in this regard. You should be on the lookout for one warning signal in particular. If a company increases the useful life of an asset, or class of assets, this spreads out the depreciation charges over a longer period of time. Thus, if the change is unreasonable, it has the effect of artificially decreasing depreciation expense and, as a consequence, increasing earnings. Depreciation methods and their effects on profits will be discussed in Chapter 9, but for now, it is enough to know that changes in depreciation methods and/or the estimated useful lives of fixed assets need to be fully explained. You will find this information in the notes to the financial statements in the annual report.

The fixed assets valuation issue, historical versus market value is generally viewed in a more positive light. Many financial commentators feel that the recorded book value (historical cost) of fixed assets, the method used for balance sheet presentations, tends to undervalue these assets over time. Well-maintained, up-to-date, serviceable assets, even though fully depreciated, can have substantial value and may even have greatly appreciated in value. Thus, depending on the particular circumstances of a given company, it may be that the balance sheet numbers for fixed assets understate their true value. These often are referred to as *hidden assets,* for little or no mention of this phenomenon appears in an annual report. Analyst investment research reports and articles in the financial press are the usual sources of this kind of information.

Nonphysical Assets

A number of *nonphysical* company assets are considered intangible assets, e.g., patents, contracts, trademarks and various types of deferred charges. In the case of the latter, these represent an outlay of funds for an activity that will benefit the company for several years. Accounting convention permits these expenditures to be capitalized as a noncurrent asset and their value amortized over time, in similar fashion to a fixed asset that is depreciated. In relative terms, these intangibles usually do not involve large numbers in the balance sheet. However, there is a species of intangible assets that is important and somewhat controversial. Purchased goodwill, or just goodwill, represents, to the acquiring company, the cost in excess of the fair value of the net assets (equity) of the acquired company. Multiple terms are employed to describe this item in a company's balance sheet. ABC's statement uses the phrase "Excess of cost over net assets acquired."

An acquisition-minded company is likely to generate a substantial amount of purchased goodwill in its balance sheet. You should be aware of the following consequences of this phenomenon:

1. Goodwill must be amortized by annual charges to earnings (through the income statement).

2. Some financial professionals tend to be uncomfortable with a relatively large amount of goodwill on the balance sheet. Only time will tell if the acquisition price paid was really fair value.

3. The goodwill will have been paid for in cash, stock and/or borrowed funds. The return to the company will be realized only if it is able to turn the acquisition into productive earnings.

4. Conservative analysis, include bankers in this classification, will reduce shareholders' equity by the amount of intangible assets, which includes goodwill, to arrive at an equity base referred to as tangible net worth. Depending on a company's capital structure, this often results in a very weak equity position when measured in this conservative manner.

☐ TOTAL ASSET TURNOVER

The last number in the asset section of the balance sheet is the total asset figure, quite logically the sum of current and noncurrent assets. The asset turnover ratio, which is a comparison of the amount of net sales produced by a company's average total asset base, is an indicator of the efficient use of assets. Industry characteristics will influence this ratio, but the higher the ratio, the greater the efficiency of a company's assets. ABC's 1991 asset turnover ratio would be calculated as follows:

1. Net sales ÷ Average total assets = Asset turnover ratio (x)
2. 1991 Net sales = $533,814
3. 1991 Average total assets:

   1990: $261,119 + 1991: $324,175 = $585,294 ÷ 2 = $292,647

4. $533,814 ÷ $292,647 = 1.8$x$

It should be obvious that those companies with a need for a heavy investment in fixed assets will tend to have lower ratios. When we prepare a spreadsheet (see Exhibit 8.1) on ABC's balance sheet at the end of this chapter, you will note that it has a relatively small investment in property, plant and equipment, only 18 percent of total assets in 1991. This low total asset amount translates into a fairly high asset turnover ratio. It now is appropriate to look at those aspects of a company's long-term liabilities that, for the most part, contribute funds to support the permanent working capital needs and noncurrent assets previously discussed.

□ LONG-TERM LIABILITIES

The main components of long-term liabilities generally consist of long-term debt and deferred income taxes. This is true of ABC's balance sheet and that of many other companies. Other long-term obligations could include such items as unearned, accrued or deferred income (deferred credits) and warranties. These are not true debt liabilities; they fall more into the category of performance obligations. Conservative analysts, however, would argue that if a company stopped operating, it would owe these amounts if the company could not provide the goods and services that it was obligated to provide. Generally, other long-term liabilities are not material.

Before I focus on long-term debt, a brief explanation of deferred income taxes is warranted. Simply stated, temporary differences between tax and financial statement reporting create the deferred taxes account. Some financial commentators take a rather benign view of this liability and think of deferred taxes as an almost permanent circumstance. The conservative approach, however, views deferred taxes as a true liability and also would include this item in any calculation of long-term debt. As expressed in annual reports, corporate practice varies. Most companies, however, choose not to include deferred income taxes in their debt calculations.

□ DEBT: NOW YOU SEE IT, NOW YOU DON'T!

Just what then is long-term debt? The answer to this question is not so simple as it appears. ABC's balance sheet, as well as that of most other companies, clearly indicates an entry for long-term debt in its liabilities section. True to form, however, corporate financial reporting practices tend to complicate matters. For some financial professionals, long-term debt is synonymous with debt. Therefore, in annual report usage, the use of the word *debt* could be used interchangeably with *long-term debt*.

For others, a company's debt is equivalent to its total liabilities, as in the component of the debt ratio, which compares total liabilities to total assets. In this instance, the terms *liability* and *debt* are synonymous. This means, however, that nondebt liabilities such as accounts payable, accrued expenses, income taxes payable, etc., also are considered *debts*. Adding to this confusion, in annual report presentations, is the lack of definition as to just how a company computes its debt, i.e., what items on and off the balance sheet are included.

This lack of precision in definition is important. The use of debt is critical to most companies' financial condition and performance. This phenomenon is widely recognized and accepted. In an annual report, the results of the various debt indicators will be discussed at some length. What a company's management considers *debt*, however, is a key issue. You need to know how debt ratios are calculated and what components are being used in the calculations. Some annual reports provide this information, but the practice is far from universally employed. Here again, corporate practice varies considerably regarding disclosure and ratio computation methods.

Here is a solution to this problem: Do your own number-crunching and take a conservative approach. Conservative analysis would include the following in a company's debt position:

- Long-term debt
- The current portion of long-term debt and short-term borrowings found in the current liabilities
- Deferred income taxes
- Other long-term liabilities
- Redeemable preferred stock
- Noncancellable operating leases

The last two items are new to this discussion and warrant a brief explanation. Redeemable preferred stock has all the characteristics of debt and should be classified as such. Noncancellable operating leases, as opposed to capital leases that are included in long-term debt, do not appear in the balance sheet. They are referred to as *off-balance-sheet* financing because they have all the attributes of debt but do not appear in the statement. The data on operating leases are found in the notes to the financial statement. Using an accepted rule-of-thumb estimate, you can consider two-thirds of the amount indicated for operating leases as long-term debt (the other one-third represents interest expense). As you will see in the case of ABC, operating leases often are critical to a company's operations and can represent a sizable debtlike obligation.

☐ USING RATIOS TO MEASURE FINANCIAL LEVERAGE

Financial leverage refers to a company's use of debt, as opposed to equity, to support its assets. The astute use of debt increases the resources available to a company for growth and greater profitability.

Leveraging, however, requires the company to maintain a good debt-paying record, and the sources of financing will carefully examine a company's debt capacity through a variety of financial analysis techniques.

Financial reporting is sensitive to this scrutiny by creditors, lenders and investors; as a consequence, a company's financial communications, which include the annual report, attempt to put the company's debt position in the best possible light. Those who have lent or invested money in a company generally have a different, more skeptical perspective.

Before we explore the principal debt ratios generally mentioned in an annual report, it is worthwhile illustrating this disparity in perspectives on debt by analyzing ABC's position as follows. On the left, various debt components are listed. The first column of figures represents how *debt* is expressed in ABC'S annual report, and the second column represents a conservative analyst's viewpoint (1991 figures):

	ABC Corporation Annual Report	*Conservative Analysis*
Short-term borrowing	$ 704	$ 704
Current portion of long-term debt	736	736
Long-term debt (including capital leases)	30,126	30,126
Deferred income taxes	—	24,000
Other long-term liabilities	—	—
Redeemable preferred stock	—	—
Noncancellable operating leases	—	20,000
Total debt	$31,566	$75,566

In view of ABC's previously mentioned small investment in fixed assets, it is not surprising that the corporation carries approximately $30 million in noncancellable operating leases. This data would be found in the notes section of its annual report. ABC has elected to lease rather than to purchase a relatively large amount of its required plant and equipment. Thus, the conservative analyst adds two-thirds of the operating lease amount (some analysts would use the whole amount) to ABC's debt obligations and also includes the deferred taxes amount. If other long-term liabilities and/or redeemable preferred stock were present in ABC's financial position, these, too, would be classified as debt. In certain instances, companies do not include short-term borrowings, and sometimes even the current portion of long-term debt, in total debt. There is a lot of room for maneuvering on this issue. The point should be quite clear that unless the annual report presentation clearly indicates what is *debt*, it would be unwise to take the related ratios and narrative at face value.

☐ THE SOLVENCY RATIOS

The solvency ratios, which provide different perspectives on a company's debt position, most often used in annual report presentations are the debt, debt-equity and capitalization ratios. A related indicator, the interest coverage ratio, is discussed within the context of the income statement in Chapter 9. Applying these ratios to ABC's 1991 balance sheet will give you a practical lesson in how these measurements of debt are computed.

The Debt Ratio

The debt ratio, which indicates the percentage of assets supported by liabilities as opposed to the owners' equity, is arrived at in the following manner:

$$\text{Total liabilities:} \quad \$130,889$$
$$\text{Total assets:} \quad \$324,175$$
$$\text{Debt ratio:} \quad \frac{\$130,889}{\$324,175} = 40\%$$

The lower the percentage, the less dependent the company is on financial leverage. You should note that it would not be appropriate to further refine this ratio by using the conservative analysis total debt figure. Because the debtlike operating lease amount has no corresponding or matching asset, its inclusion in the ratio's calculation would be distortive. With the other solvency ratios, however, this problem does not exist, and it is worthwhile putting the standard calculations to the test of the more strict interpretation of debt.

The Debt-Equity Ratio

The debt-equity ratio, defined here as a comparison of total liabilities to shareholders' equity, measures how much the creditors and lenders have put into the company versus what the shareholders have committed. The lower the percentage, the greater the company's financial safety and operating freedom. ABC's 1991 debt-equity ratios, applying both standard and conservative analysis, are computed as follows:

Total liabilities: $130,889

Shareholders' equity: $193,286

Debt-equity ratio: $\dfrac{\$130,889}{\$193,286} = 68\%$

Adjusted total liabilities: $130,889 + $20,000 = $150,889

Adjusted debt-equity ratio: $\dfrac{\$150,889}{\$193,286} = 78\%$

Even when the conservative approach to the calculation of this ratio is used, ABC still shows a comfortable margin of shareholders' invested funds over those provided by liability sources.

The Capitalization Ratio

The capitalization ratio indicates the makeup of a company's permanent capital, defined here as long-term debt plus equity, or otherwise referred to as its capitalization. The lower the percentage, the smaller the debt component and the larger the equity portion. ABC's 1991 capitalization ratios, standard and adjusted, reflect the following results:

Long-term debt: $30,126 + $736 = $30,862

Shareholders' equity: $193,286

Capitalization ratio: $\dfrac{\$30,862}{\$30,862 + \$193,286} = 14\%$

Adjusted long-term debt:
$$\begin{array}{r} \$30,126 \\ 736 \\ 24,000 \\ \underline{20,000} \\ \$74,862 \end{array}$$

Adjusted capitalization ratio: $\dfrac{74,862}{\$74,862 + \$193,286} = 28\%$

Again, ABC comes through with flying colors. By either measurement, the company registers a low dependence on debt and, therefore, enjoys a strong equity position.

This discussion of the solvency ratios concludes the review of the balance sheet's liability section. Before reviewing various aspects of shareholders' equity, however, some unusual statement entries warrant clarification. Only one of these items appears in the ABC balance sheet.

☐ SPECIAL ITEMS

Commitment and Contingencies

Three items of a special nature can appear in the liabilities section of the balance sheet but do not appear to have a direct liability connection:

1. Commitment and contingencies,
2. Minority interest and
3. Redeemable preferred stock.

As seen in the ABC statement, there is a notation for *commitments and contingencies* but no corresponding amount. These are potential liabilities and/or obligations that are not quantifiable in accounting terms but could have an impact on the financial position of the company in the future. The circumstances of these commitments and contingencies are discussed in a note to the financial statements. This information can be extremely complex (lengthy explanations) or routine (short, boilerplate text). Being able to determine the difference is important. This subject matter will be discussed in detail in Chapter 12 where key notes to a company's financial statements will be reviewed.

Minority Interest

Another item, *minority interest,* is seen only in balance sheets of those companies with investments in unconsolidated subsidiaries that are not wholly owned. ABC has no investments of this nature. You may remember from the discussion in Chapter 6 that in the process of consolidation, the majority investor company absorbs 100 percent of the net asset value of the investee company. If the majority investor owns only 80 percent, however, the minority shareholders' interest must be recognized. This is accomplished in financial statement accounting by recording a minority interest on the liability side of the investor company's balance sheet. If this was not done, the assets of the investor company would be overstated. While opinion differs on this issue, many observers, myself included, consider this a *balancing item*. It is not a true liability because there is no mandatory payment of interest, dividends or principal. The amount usually is insignificant, so any argument over its precise classification really is academic.

Redeemable Preferred Stock

The last item, *redeemable preferred stock*, often is found in a kind of *no-man's-land* between the liability and equity sections in the balance sheet of a company that has issued this type of security. You need not share this financial statement formatting ambivalence. These securities must be redeemed by an issuing company in a manner similar to the repayment of debt. Redeemable preferred stock with its mandatory redemption requirements is a form of debt. It has more of the characteristics of debt than equity and, therefore, as indicated previously, should be included in the calculations of a company's debt.

□ SHAREHOLDERS' EQUITY

If you reconfigure the balance sheet equation, assets = liabilities + equity, you can easily determine that shareholders' equity is the owners' piece of the business, the difference between assets and liabilities:

$$Equity = Assets - Liabilities$$

ABC's equity section in its balance sheet presentation is quite standard. In recent years, however, some special items have appeared that need to be explained. First, a few comments about the terminology applied to this component of the balance sheet. *Book value* and *net worth* are expressions that generally do not appear in an annual report presentation but are used quite frequently in financial writing. These terms are synonymous with shareholders' equity, as the connotations of these words indicate. To a lesser degree, the term *net assets* also is used as an equivalent for equity.

The first component of the equity section is the entry or entries for capital stock, the ownership shares of a company. A company can issue preferred and common stock. The latter applies to ABC's situation and is the most generally used equity security. As the term implies, preferred stockholders take precedence over common stockholders with respect to the receipt of dividends and the distribution of assets if the company is liquidated. Also, the dividend rate is fixed and dividends are cumulative for preferred stock.

Additional paid-in capital simply records the amount of money paid by shareholders over the amount designated as par value for a company's common stock. Par value is the stated value of common stock and is used for legal purposes. The reason for the general practice of setting a low par value is twofold: Incorporation taxes may apply to this amount, and, for appearances' sake, no company wants the market price of its stock selling under par. In the case of ABC (1991), 15,254,695 shares issued and outstanding at a penny per share par value means that $153,000 (in round figures) is recorded as the investment in common stock. The difference between this amount and additional paid-in capital of $83,917,000 is $83,764,000 (in round figures). Simple math thus indicates that investors, on a per-share basis, paid $.01 par value plus $5.49 ($83,764,000 ÷ 15,254,695 = $5.49) for ABC's common stock.

Retained earnings, as the term implies, are the profits that have been kept in the business as permanent working capital and/or fixed investment. Profits build up retained earnings, and it is from this account that dividends are paid to shareholders.

□ ADJUSTMENTS TO THE EQUITY POSITION

Treasury stock, foreign currency translation and an Employee Stock Ownership Plan (ESOP) obligation guarantee represent three special items that sometimes appear as adjustments to a company's equity account. In the case of ABC, its operations have not occasioned any of these events, and its equity position format is routine.

When a company purchases its own stock in the open market, and it is not retired, the stock no longer is outstanding but is held as treasury stock. This circumstance requires that the purchase value of this stock appear as a reduction to the equity account. Acquisition plans, employee stock option plans and the existence of convertible securities are the more transparent reasons for a company to maintain treasury stock.

Less obvious, but also cause for stock repurchases are these corporate considerations:

1. Fending off takeover attempts,

2. Preparing to go private,
3. Hyping per-share earnings,
4. Perceiving the market as undervaluing its stock,
5. Attempting to support a stable stock price.

A U.S. company's financial statements are expressed in U.S. dollars. Those of its foreign branches, subsidiaries and affiliates are in some foreign currency. Consolidating all these financials poses a problem because of the volatility of international exchange rates. As the dollar gains and loses strength, unrealized gains and losses in the translation of a company's foreign operations occur. Rather than pass these gains and losses, caused entirely by exchange fluctuations, through the income statement, which would destabilize reported earnings, they are reflected as an adjustment to the equity account.

Finally, when an ESOP borrows the money to buy a company's stock and the company guarantees the loan, an equity adjustment will be recorded. The company's balance sheet reflects a *guaranteed ESOP obligation* as a component of its long-term debt. A like amount is reflected as a reduction of shareholders' equity. As the ESOP loan is repaid, the liability obligation and the equity adjustment amounts are reduced accordingly.

□ USING A SPREADSHEET TO ANALYZE A BALANCE SHEET

The spreadsheet illustrated in Exhibit 8.1 is an abbreviated example of a homemade approach to analyzing balance sheets. You do not have to possess sophisticated financial analysis skills to successfully use this tool. Simple math skills, some columned accounting paper, a #3 pencil (a number-cruncher's favorite) and a calculator will do. If you use computers, you probably are already aware of the wonders that spreadsheet software can perform in this regard.

What will a spreadsheet tell you? A spreadsheet is the financial equivalent of a medical X ray. It will help you understand the structure of the balance sheet, its strengths and weaknesses, and you will be able to track changes that may reveal trends. Also, by applying a standardized analysis, you can make comparisons between companies in the same business and better appreciate the financial profiles of companies in different industry sectors.

Remember to look at three to five years of statement information to obtain meaningful trend data. For illustration purposes, the

EXHIBIT 8.1 Spreadsheet Illustration—Balance Sheet—The ABC Corporation

THE ABC CORPORATION
BALANCE SHEETS AS OF DEC. 31ST

(A)	B 1990 AMOUNT	C 1.00	D +/- %	E 1991 AMOUNT	F 1.00	G +/- %
			(AMOUNTS IN THOUSANDS)			
ASSETS						
① Cash/Invested Funds	18,482	.07	—	92,252	.29	
② Trade Receivables	64,768	.25	—	72,335	.22	+ 12%
③ Inventories	91,639	.35	—	73,451	.23	− 20%
④ Prepaids & Other	25,097	.10	—	23,968	.07	
Total Current Assets	199,986	.77	—	262,006	.81	+ 31%
⑤ Investments	—	—	—	—	—	
⑥ Fixed Assets	46,652	.18	—	59,929	.18	+ 27%
⑦ Intangibles	3,703	.01	—	2,240	.01	
⑧ Other Assets	10,778	.04	—	—	—	
Total Assets	261,119	1.00	—	324,175	1.00	+ 24%
LIABILITIES						
⑨ Borrowed Funds	—	—	—	1,440	—	
⑩ Accounts Payable	32,806	.13	—	29,304	.09	− 11%
⑪ Accruals	19,978	.08	—	37,622	.12	+ 88%
⑫ Taxes	4,715	.01	—	8,397	.03	
⑬ Other Current Liab.	713	—	—	—	—	
Total Current Liabilities	58,212	.22	—	76,763	.24	+ 32%
⑭ Long-Term Debt	81,045	.31	—	30,126	.09	− 63%
⑮ Other Liabilities	13,063	.05	—	24,000	.07	
Total Liabilities	152,320	.58	—	130,889	.40	− 14%
⑯ Minority Interest	—	—	—	—	—	
EQUITY						
⑰ Shareholders' Equity	108,799	.42	—	193,286	.60	+ 78%
Total Liab. & S.E.	261,119	1.00	—	324,175	1.00	+ 24%

FIGURE 8.2 Coded Balance Sheets for Spreadsheet Analysis—The ABC Corporation

Years ended December 31 (in thousands, except per-share amounts		*1991*	*1990*
ASSETS	**CURRENTS ASSETS:**		
	Cash and cash equivalents ①	$ 92,252	$ 18,482
	Accounts receivable, net of allowance for doubtful accounts of $5,749 in 1991, $3,567 in 1990 ②	72,335	64,768
	Inventories ③	73,451	91,639
	Prepaid expenses ④	18,036	20,416
	Other current assets	5,932	4,681
	Total current assets	262,006	199,986
	Plant, property and equipment	83,236	63,729
	Accumulated depreciation and amortization	(23,307)	(17,077)
	Net plant, property and equipment ⑥	59,929	46,652
	Excess of cost over net assets acquired ⑦	2,240	3,703
	Other assets ⑧	–	10,778
	Total assets	$324,175	$261,119
LIABILITIES AND SHAREHOLDERS' EQUITY	**CURRENT LIABILITIES:**		
	Short-term borrowings ⑨	$ 704	$ –
	Accounts payable ⑩	29,304	32,806
	Accrued salaries, wages and employee benefits ⑪	10,240	5,424
	Other accrued liabilities	27,382	14,554
	Income taxes payable ⑫	8,397	4,715
	Current portion of long-term debt ⑨	736	713
	Total current liabilities	76,763	58,212
	Long-term debt ⑭	30,126	81,045
	Deferred income taxes ⑮	24,000	13,063
	Commitments and contingencies		
	SHAREHOLDERS' EQUITY:		
	Common stock, par value $.01; 30,000,000 shares authorized; 15,254,695 shares issues and outstanding in 1991; 11,628,334 in 1990	153	117
	Additional paid-in capital	83,917	34,533
	Retained earnings	109,216	74,149
	Total shareholders' equity ⑰	193,286	108,799
	Total liabilities and shareholders' equity	$324,175	$261,119

The accompanying notes are an integral part of the financial statements.

spreadsheet for ABC covers only two years; 1990 is the base year. You could go back in time and choose another base year to generate a three- to five-year perspective. This spreadsheet has a standardized classification of balance sheet accounts in column A. As you can see, Exhibit 8.2 is a reproduction of ABC's balance sheet. The various account amounts are coded. The circled numbers correspond to the line items in column A of the spreadsheet. This simple procedure has a purpose—to remind you from one year to the next of your classification of the balance sheet item, thus ensuring a consistent, comparable analysis. For example, ABC's cash and cash equivalents and marketable securities, if there ever are any, would be coded as 1 on the balance sheet and the amounts totaled in line 1, columns B and E of the spreadsheet. To simplify things, line items in column A such as Prepaids and other, Other assets, Accruals, Other current liabilities and Other liabilities are used to aggregate less critical balance sheet numbers.

Columns C and F and D and G represent what financial professionals refer to as vertical and horizontal analysis, respectively. Do not be intimidated by this fancy-sounding terminology. Vertical analysis is nothing more than determining the compositional nature, expressed as a decimal, of the individual parts of the balance sheet's *total footings*, i.e., the totals for assets and liabilities/equity. Horizontal analysis simply measures the interannual changes, expressed as a percentage increase or decrease, in those balance sheet accounts you wish to monitor.

What can you learn about ABC from vertical analysis? Even though the time frame is limited, the numerical indicators in columns C and F portray a very liquid balance sheet with current assets accounting for more than three-quarters of total assets in both years. In addition, in 1991, the quality of current assets improved significantly as the dependence on inventories dropped and, while possibly only a temporary situation, cash and invested funds rose dramatically. ABC's low investment in fixed assets is confirmed by a relatively small percentage, 18 percent, of total assets. The company's financial leverage has reversed itself in the two years under review. In 1990, total liabilities exceeded equity, 58 percent versus 42 percent, respectively, while in 1991, this relationship shows equity (60 percent) supporting more assets than liabilities (40 percent).

While this comparison is limited to two years, which is inadequate, you can envision from this illustration how interannual changes (horizontal analysis) can help you monitor a company's financial health. In this case, our attention is focused on column G. Among other observations, the growth in current liabilities was matched by a similar expansion of current assets. This meant that ABC was able to maintain a consistent 3.4 to 1 current ratio for both years, which, as noted previously, involved a significant increase in sales volume. This is a good sign that the company's expanding activities, especially its working capital position, is being well managed. ABC's asset base grew a significant 24 percent, while liabilities, particularly long-term debt, actually decreased. The company appears to have converted a substantial portion of its long-term debt into equity.

Needless to say, it should be evident from this very limited illustration just how valuable spreadsheet analysis can be to better understand the financial condition and performance of a company. We will revisit this technique and apply it to the income statement, which will be examined in the following chapter.

9

MEASURING PROFITABILITY

☐ THE STATEMENT OF INCOME

First, a few words of explanation regarding the diversity of financial reporting terminology. I will use the term *income statement* to identify the financial statement more formally referred to as the statement of income, statement of earnings, statement of operations or statement of operating results. I have discarded the habit of using the term *P&L* (for profit and loss statement), although many financial professionals still use this vernacular reference. The income statement records a company's operating performance by reflecting sources of income and the various costs and expenses, gains and losses, which result in a final net income (loss) figure. This amount is transferred, net of any preferred dividend payments, to the retained earnings account in the equity section of the balance sheet at a company's fiscal year-end.

As an introduction to the income statement, it is important to remember that most companies use the accrual method for their financial reporting. Thus, a company's revenues are recognized when they are realized (goods shipped or services rendered) and expenses are recognized when they are incurred. This accounting principle means that the flow of accounting events does not necessarily coincide with the actual receipt and disbursement of cash. The statement of cash flows, reviewed in the next chapter, gives you that information. The income

EXHIBIT 9.1 Consolidated Statements of Income—The ABC Corporation

Years ended December 31 (in thousands, except per-share amounts)

	1991	1990	1989
Net sales	$533,814	$456,520	$412,721
Cost of sales	360,439	344,334	295,803
Gross profit	173,375	112,186	116,918
Selling and marketing expenses	71,596	66,354	55,538
General and administrative expenses	28,911	32,889	22,705
Research and development expenses	18,441	16,944	15,693
Total operating expenses	118,948	116,187	93,936
Operating income (loss)	54,427	(4,001)	22,982
Interest income	4,804	1,490	950
Interest expense	(5,966)	(7,572)	(2,314)
Other expense, net	(1,694)	(1,497)	(686)
Income (loss) before provision (benefit) for income taxes	51,571	(11,580)	20,932
Provision (benefit) for income taxes	16,504	(4,111)	5,861
Net income (loss)	$ 35,067	$ (7,469)	$ 15,071
Net income (loss) per share	2.86	(0.64)	1.28
Weighted average common shares outstanding	12,265	11,580	11,743

The accompanying notes are an integral part of the financial statements.

statement measures profitability not cash flow, and the two concepts are not synonymous. Do not confuse profits with "money in the bank."

One last general observation: The words *income, profits* and *earnings* are used interchangeably in financial communications, including annual reports, and I will conform to this practice.

□ THE FORMAT CAN MAKE A DIFFERENCE

Two different formats are used to present the income statement—the multistep and the singlestep. The multistep is used most often in annual reports, which, as you will see, is to your benefit. The multistep approach, which is illustrated by ABC's statement of income in Exhibit 9.1, allows you to pinpoint the results of operations at critical junctures as you view the flow of business by management functions. These critical junctures are measured by comparing the various components of the income statement to net sales (see the spreadsheet in Exhibit 9.3 on page 89).

Gross profit reflects how well the purchasing and production elements are performing. ABC's format disclosure provides additional help by breaking out sales and marketing costs from what most companies report as selling, general and administrative (SG&A) expenses as an aggregate amount. ABC Corporation's form of presentation helps you to independently measure the effectiveness of the selling function and general overhead expense as components of total operating expenses.

After deducting these expenses, operating income is revealed. After the net effect of interest expense and other income/expense, a pretax income figure is produced, which many financial commentators consider a better indicator of earnings than the after-tax income number. A company will use whatever leeway it has to lessen the burden of taxes, which often includes some rather complex maneuverings, to produce a net income or *bottom line* figure. Thus, the net income figure can be heavily influenced by tax as opposed to normal operating considerations.

I have reconfigured ABC's multistep income statement into a single-step format in Exhibit 9.2. This form of presentation, which groups revenue sources and expenses into two major groups, does not easily reveal gross profit nor operating income. Neither does this format facilitate the understanding of the flow of operations as described in the multistep approach. Obviously, the components of the single-step statement can be juggled around to provide the same information (one of the uses of a spreadsheet), but multistep presentations are more readily understood and are worksavers when it comes to number-crunching. I will use ABC's income statement, therefore, to explain in more detail what you need to know about the various components of this financial report.

EXHIBIT 9.2 Single-Step Format for ABC Statement of Income

The ABC Corporation
Statement of Income 1991

Revenues:	
Net sales	$533,814
Interest income	4,804
Total revenues	538,618
Cost and expenses:	
Cost of sales	360,439
Selling and marketing expenses	71,596
General and administrative expenses	28,911
Research and development expenses	18,441
Interest expense	5,966
Other expense, net	1,694
Total costs and expenses	487,047
Income before taxes	51,571
Provision for taxes	(16,504)
Net income	$ 35,067

□ SALES – COST OF SALES = GROSS PROFIT

Sales

Annual report presentations tend to focus on earnings. However, quoting respected financial adviser Charles Allmon (*Growth Stock Outlook*), "Over the long term companies can grow no faster than revenues." Sales growth, therefore, is an important profitability indicator. Because of its importance, you should be concerned *how* sales grow. In this instance, the extent of ABC's disclosure regarding sales in its annual report is, unfortunately, typical of most companies' presentations. Interannual percentage increases and/or decreases, accompanied by a generalized narrative, usually are found in the management discussion and analysis section (see Chapter 5). What you really want to know, however, is what were the underlying causes for a growth or decline in sales. Some companies provide these details in their annual reports; most do not. Using ABC's 1990–91 comparison of sales, let's look at the kind of supplemental information that would be most helpful:

	1990	*1991*	*Percentage Change*
Sales:	$456,520	$533,814	+16.9%
Sales growth factor:			
Volume:			+ 9.8%
Price:			+ 4.0%
Acquisition:			+ 1.5%
Foreign exchange:			+ 1.6%

As a rule, all sales increases are good, but some are qualitatively better than others. Volume growth is quite obviously the best contributor. Price increases, especially those above the general level of inflation, have their limits, as does sales expansion from acquisitions. Exchange-rate movements affecting foreign operations are outside the control of management. If ABC's healthy 1991 sales increase was caused more by price and acquisition factors, or, even more important, a pattern of sales growth depended on these factors, you would have to be concerned about the sustainability of sales growth at the high level indicated.

Also, you should be concerned about any concentration of sales with one or a limited number of customers. If any single customer accounts for more than ten percent of total sales, accounting rules require this to be mentioned in a note to the financial statements. Obviously, an exaggerated dependency on the fortunes of another company adds an element of uncertainty to the selling company's future.

Finally, a company's sales mix can affect a company's profitability. Different products or product lines carry different profit margins. If a high-margin item accounts for a greater percentage of total sales, profits from the same amount of sales will improve. We will revisit this subject when we discuss the business segment information note in Chapter 12.

Cost of Sales

This important cost item, sometimes expressed as cost of products sold, represents the expense of producing a company's inventory, i.e., the cost of raw materials, labor and production overhead (depreciation, utilities, taxes, administrative expenses, etc.) used to produce finished products. It is relatively easy to relate this definition to manufacturers. For retailers, distributors and wholesalers, their cost of sales is basically the purchase of merchandise for resale. Service businesses do not have a cost of sales, but sometimes use the term *cost of services* to indicate operating costs. A comprehensive financial analysis of the cost of sales' effect on earnings is beyond the scope of this chapter. I feel compelled, however, to make you aware of certain aspects related to the calculation of the cost of sales that have significant impact on this important income statement account. To be specific, these involve inventory valuations and depreciation expense.

A company's choice of its inventory valuation method, which is a fairly complex issue, will impact significantly on the amount of the cost of sales. The three most commonly employed methods are first-in, first-out (FIFO) method; last-in, first-out (LIFO) method and the average method. Some companies use a mix of these methods. The key point to remember is that the FIFO approach lowers the cost of sales amount, thereby generating a higher gross profit figure (sales – cost of sales = gross profit). The LIFO approach has the reverse effect of FIFO, i.e., it increases the cost of sales amount and thus generates a lower gross profit figure. As the term implies, the average method is a compromise position between LIFO and FIFO. The LIFO method is considered a more conservative approach, the most realistic in an inflationary environment, that tends to understate earnings. In making intercompany comparisons, make sure to read the inventory accounting policy notes to the companies' financial statements to determine the comparability, or lack of, of their profit positions.

Two aspects of depreciation expense deserve clarification. The first deals with the format of the income statement. Some companies choose to disclose depreciation expense as a separate line item in their statements. This practice creates a small problem. How do you compare the cost of sales and resulting gross profit figures from this kind of statement presentation to the presentations of the majority of companies whose cost of sales is included in depreciation? You simply add back the separately disclosed depreciation expense amount to the cost of sales figure. More than likely, most companies, certainly manufacturers, have depreciable assets that are used for production and, therefore, are allocable to the cost of sales. Without this adjustment, the cost of sales will be understated, thus overstating gross profit. Also, the income statement would reflect a relatively large other expense item in operating expenses.

Secondly, just as there are alternative inventory valuation methods, companies can choose from a selection of depreciation methods. For financial reporting purposes, however, the vast majority of companies use the straight-line method. This approach spreads out the depreciation expense over the useful life of the asset, which tends to minimize the expense in the income statement, resulting in higher earnings.

Companies using one of the accelerated methods, more often applied to tax reporting than to financial statement reporting, maximize the depreciation expense effect on the income statement, resulting in lower earnings (and lower taxes). These companies, by lowering earnings, are thought of as conservative, tending to understate their profitability. As a practical matter, however, you rarely will see an annual report in which a company is using anything but straight-line depreciation.

ABC's cost of sales as a percentage of net sales dropped dramatically in 1991 to 68 percent from an average of more than 73 percent for the previous two years. According to remarks in the management discussion and analysis section of its annual report, significant improvements in ABC's manufacturing processes and lower component costs account for this reduction in the cost of sales.

Gross Profit

Sometimes referred to as *gross margin*, this is the first key profitability indicator in a company's income statement. Its importance cannot be overestimated. Gross profits provide the resources to cover all the other costs and expenses of the company. The greater and more stable the gross profit margin, the greater potential there is for profitability.

The combination of increased sales and a lower cost of sales has provided a healthy boost to ABC's gross profit margin, improving from a previous two-year average of approximately 27 percent to 32 percent in 1991.

□ GROSS PROFIT – OPERATING EXPENSES = OPERATING INCOME

Operating Expenses

As mentioned previously, ABC Corporation's income statement format breaks out its selling and marketing expenses from the more generally used form of including them in one operating expense account, usually identified as selling, general and administrative (SG&A) expenses. In addition, because ABC operates in a technical field, its research and development (R&D) expenses are important to the company's success and are, therefore, shown separately (highlighted) rather than being buried in an aggregate number for SG&A.

A comparison of these individual components of ABC's operating expenses to net sales reflects extremely favorable, albeit brief, trends. For example, sales for the 1989–91 period have increased by $121,093,000, a percentage growth rate of more than 29 percent. And yet, selling and marketing expenses have remained stable at 13 percent of sales. General and administrative expenses, which tend to balloon in high growth situations, actually have dropped a notch from 6 percent in 1989 to 5 percent in 1991. True to its commitment to technological excellence, ABC has maintained its R&D expenditures at a steady 4 percent of sales throughout the period. Quite a performance, and one that translates into an operating income margin of 10 percent, almost double that of 1989.

Other income and expenses, generally of a nonmaterial character, except for possibly interest expense, are netted out from the operating income amount, resulting in income before the provision for income taxes, or pretax income. Before proceeding to the bottom line, however, it is worthwhile to explain a variety of unusual or special items that sometimes appear in income statement presentations.

☐ SPECIAL INCOME STATEMENT ITEMS

A number of unusual items can appear in an income statement. I think of these as falling into two distinct categories: recurring and nonrecurring. The former would include minority interest and equity in earnings of affiliates. These entries represent a reduction of income and additional income, respectively. The amounts generally are not very significant. The minority interest in earnings account in the income statement is directly related to the minority interest discussed as a balance sheet item in Chapter 8. Just as this latter entry recognizes a minority participation in the assets of a consolidating parent company, so, too, does the income statement entry recognize the minority interest's share of the consolidated earnings. Here again, as was the case with the balance sheet, it is a *balancing entry*. In the income statement of the minority interest company, an entry would appear recognizing this source of income as equity in earnings of affiliates.

Of a more serious nature are unusual or extraordinary items that can add to or subtract from income. Whatever the case, these items affect the quality of earnings by distorting the normal or recurring earnings pattern of a company. One factor used in qualifying a company's earnings as *good quality* involves the absence of nonrecurring or nonoperating income, which artificially inflates profits. These unusual items must be recognized as such in any interannual comparison of results and in the calculation of the relevant ratios. It is important to read the related notes to the financial statements on these entries to fully appreciate their impact on a company's performance.

Many times companies attempt to prop up faltering earnings with income items generally considered outside their *normal* operations. For example, during the 1990–91 period, the McDonald's Corporation's revenues and profits were being squeezed by increasing competition. Analysts pointed out that it was precisely at this time that McDonald's starting selling company-owned restaurants to its franchisees at an accelerated pace. As reported in *Forbes* (September 16, 1991), the company considered the gains from the sales of restaurants as normal operating income, i.e., not as unusual or extraordinary income. One skeptical financial analyst, Robert Gay of Donaldson, Lufkin & Jenrette, characterized this approach as "essentially . . . selling off shareholder wealth."

When a company decides to discontinue a line of business, this must be reported separately from continuing operations in the income statement. You can reasonably assume that discontinued operations represent a problematical situation for a company. Anything that is making money, i.e., performing well, generally is not discontinued. Do not assume that the use of the past tense of the word *discontinued* means that the problem is history. Generally accepted accounting principles allow a company to record discontinued operations as such on the basis of an *adopted plan* as opposed to actual disposition. In fact, the costs and risks associated with disposing of these operations may plague a company for an extended period of time.

A change in a company's accounting policies can affect earnings either positively or negatively. The consequences of such actions are explained in the notes to the financial statements, and their occurrence is always identified in the auditors' report. In most instances, the impact is not that material, but it does represent another nonrecurring event that affects the normal reporting of a company's earnings.

□ GETTING DOWN TO THE BOTTOM LINE

Income before the Provision for Income Taxes

Picking up where we left off in the review of the statement of income, the pretax income figure is another of those key junctures on the road to the bottom line. Because of the nonoperating, diverse nature of the techniques being used by companies to avoid and/or minimize taxes, the pretax income figure often is considered by many financial professionals as the most reliable indicator of a company's profit performance. Thus, this figure often is substituted for the net income figure used in the various profitability ratios and indicators. ABC's pretax income comparison to net sales rebounded from the negative results in 1990 to double (10 percent) the 1989 performance of 5 percent.

Provision for Income Taxes

Not much needs to be said about the line item for taxes. Almost everybody pays taxes, as do companies if they have pretax income. Companies also may enjoy tax benefits, as in the case of ABC in 1990, and this will appear as an addition to income. You should note that the word *provision* is purposely employed in this account caption. As presented in the income statement, these are not taxes that have been paid but an estimate of what a company expects to pay. The actual amount of taxes paid often is disclosed as supplemental information to the statement of cash flows. The difference usually is not material.

Another aspect worth noting is the calculation of the effective tax rate. This often is done for you and is disclosed in a note to the financial statements, but you can easily determine this percentage by dividing the amount for taxes by the pretax income amount. In ABC's two profitable years, 1989 and 1991, this works out to 28 percent and 32 percent, respectively. Pay attention to a company's effective tax rate, particularly when making interannual earnings comparisons, because of its obvious impact on net income.

Net Income

After the reduction of income by income taxes, we finally arrive at net income or net profit or net earnings; take your pick, for they all mean the same thing. Of course, if the income results are negative, it is interesting to note that there is only one term that is used—*net loss*. Net income is used to feed the retained earnings account. From this account, dividends are paid or the funds reinvested in the company, as permanent working capital or fixed investment. ABC's return on sales, net income compared to net sales, tripled from the 2 percent registered in 1989 to 6 percent in 1991.

□ USING RATIOS TO MEASURE A COMPANY'S EARNINGS PERFORMANCE

The gross profit, operating income, pretax income, net income and margin ratios, comparing these profit levels to net sales, have been discussed in the review of the income statement. Some or all of these generally are commented on in annual report presentations. Appearing frequently in annual reports are three other profitability ratios that compare net income to assets, equity and capital employed (a company's capitalization).

The Return on Assets (ROA) Ratio

The *return on assets* (ROA) ratio indicates the productivity of a company's assets. A high percentage implies well-managed assets. Using ABC's 1991 figures, its ROA is computed as follows:

Net income: $35,067
Average total assets: $292,647 ($261,119 + $324,175 = $585,294 ÷ 2)
Return on assets: $35,607 ÷ $292,647 = 12% ROA

The Return on Equity (ROE) Ratio

The *return on equity* (ROE) ratio measures how much the shareholders earn on their investment. For ABC, its 1991 ROE was quite high, particularly when you consider its reasonable level of financial leverage:

Net income: $35,067
Average equity: $151,043 ($108,799 + $193,286 = $302,085 ÷ 2)
Return on equity: $35,067 ÷ $151,043 = 23.2% ROE

You should be aware that in the case of the ROE ratio, some annual report presentations use beginning equity as the amount for the denominator in the return on equity formula. The more common practice is to use an average equity amount. The differing results of these two approaches can readily be seen in this illustration for ABC's 1991 ROE ratio:

	12/31/90	12/31/91
Shareholders' equity:	$108,799	$193,286
Net income:	–	$ 35,067
ROE (using $108,799 as beginning equity):		32.2%
ROE (using average equity):		23.2%

The Return on Capital Employed (ROCE) Ratio

The *return on capital employed* (ROCE) ratio expands on the ROE indicator to include, in addition to equity, borrowed funds (long-term debt, current portion of long-term debt and short-term borrowings). Long-term lenders and investors are interested in a company's ability to generate earnings from its total pool of capital, debt and equity. Here again, even by this stricter profitability measurement, ABC's 1991 performance is very good:

Net income:	$ 35,067
Average borrowed funds:	$ 56,662 ($81,758 + $31,566 ÷ 2)
Average equity:	$151,043
Return on capital employed:	$$\frac{\$35,067}{(\$56,662 + \$151,043)} = 16.9\% \text{ ROCE}$$

The Earnings Per Share (EPS) Ratio

Two earnings-related indicators receive a lot of attention from investment analysts and investors. A company's *earnings per share* (EPS) is prominently displayed in an annual report, while the other, the widely used *price-earnings,* or PE, ratio is seldom if ever mentioned. EPS indicates the dollar net income per share of common stock. The formula for EPS is simple: net income – preferred dividends ÷ the number of shares outstanding.

Most annual reports provide this calculation for you. It is perhaps worth mentioning that this indicator can improve in two ways—by increasing earnings and by decreasing the number of shares outstanding. The latter event occurs when a company buys back a significant amount of its own shares (stock repurchase plan), thus inflating EPS without the benefit of improved earnings.

The Price-Earnings (PE) Ratio

The price-earnings ratio indicates the relationship between a company's market price per share and its earnings per share. This ratio is a big favorite of the investment community. A high PE ratio is associated with companies with substantial growth potential, and, conversely, low PE ratios with slow-growth prospects. This very well-known and popular ratio is a useful yardstick for evaluating market prices but not necessarily as an indicator for evaluating the real worth of a company.

The Times Interest Earned (Interest Coverage) Ratio

In the discussion of solvency, or debt, ratios in Chapter 8, we discussed an earnings-related ratio that measures a company's debt-paying ability. This indicator, the times interest earned, or interest coverage, ratio is mentioned occasionally in annual reports. The use of the word *earned* in the ratio's description can be confusing. Think of this interest coverage ratio as *times interest expense*. This more logical expression tells us, as does the ratio, the number of times recurring income, generally adjusted pretax income, covers the amount of interest expense. Using ABC's 1991 income statement, we can calculate the ratio as follows:

Income before taxes (add back-interest expense):	$57,537
	($51,571 + $5,966)
Interest expense (include capitalized interest):	$5,966
Interest coverage ratio:	9.6x

If a company can keep current on its interest payments, it usually can maintain the confidence of its creditors and refinance principal payments. As of year-end 1991, ABC is in a very healthy position as earnings could fall almost ten times from its present level before prejudicing its ability to service its interest expense.

The discussion of operating leases in Chapter 8 indicated that it is common practice for some analysts to consider one-third of these debtlike obligations as interest expense. Thus, for the calculation of the times interest expense ratio, as well as the fixed charges ratio that follows, you should adjust the interest expense amount used in both of these calculations for this circumstance. To make the adjustments, simply add one-third of the annual operating lease rental expense to the interest expense amount.

The Fixed Charges Ratio

Seldom seen in annual reports, the fixed charges ratio is worth mentioning here. It, too, uses the same adjusted pretax income figure as the numerator for the interest coverage ratio. This figure is divided by the sum of interest expense and the current portion of long-term debt, i.e., those key obligations that a company must meet to maintain its good credit standing. Once again, ABC comes through with flying colors, at least for 1991:

Adjusted pretax income:	$57,537
Fixed charges:	$6,702
	($5,966 + $736)
Fixed charges ratio:	8.6x

☐ USING A SPREADSHEET TO ANALYZE THE INCOME STATEMENT

A spreadsheet for the income statement works the same way as the one for the balance sheet as described in Chapter 8. Exhibit 9.3 illustrates what all of the number-crunching can reveal, and Exhibit 9.4 provides you with ABC's coded statement of income. My comments on the structure of the presentation of income, costs and expenses in the income statement, earlier in this chapter, incorporated various profitability indicators that are clearly revealed in a spreadsheet's vertical analysis in columns C and F. The decimal expressions for gross profit, operating income, pretax income and net income components are the equivalent of the profit margin ratios previously mentioned.

A horizontal analysis of an income statement provides you with interannual growth rates, which are more important for the income statement than the balance sheet. Columns D (1989 figures are the base here) and G provide percentage increases and decreases for all the statement line items (if a percentage change is exaggerated or not meaningful, it is not calculated and is noted as n.c.). You also can compare items between spreadsheets. For example, ABC's sales increased 17 percent in the 1990–91 period, while receivables expanded only 12 percent and inventories actually declined a significant 20 percent. This indicates that even with a greater volume of business, ABC's management kept these important operating working capital components under control and even improved the liquidity of its current position.

Look at the behavior of ABC's various operating expenses for this same period. They really knew what they were doing! Sales grew

EXHIBIT 9.3 Spreadsheet Illustration—Income Statement—The ABC Corporation

THE ABC CORPORATION
INCOME STATEMENTS FOR 1990 - 1991

(A)	(B) 1990 AMOUNT	(C) 1.00	(D) +/- %	(E) 1991 AMOUNT	(F) 1.00	(G) +/- %
① NET SALES	456,520	1.00	+ 11%	533,814	1.00	+ 17%
② COST OF SALES	(344,334)	.75	+ 16%	(360,439)	.68	+ 5%
③ GROSS PROFIT (LOSS)	112,186	.25	- 4%	173,375	.32	+ 55%
④ SELLING/MKTG. EXPS.	(66,354)	.14	+ 19%	(71,596)	.13	+ 8%
⑤ GNL. & ADM. EXPS.	(32,889)	.07	+ 45%	(28,911)	.05	- 12%
⑥ R & D EXPS.	(16,944)	.04	+ 8%	(18,441)	.04	+ 9%
⑦ TOTAL OPERATING EXPS	(116,187)	.25	+ 24%	(118,948)	.22	+ 2%
⑧ OPERATING INCOME (LOSS)	(4,001)	.01	- 117%	54,427	.10	N.C.
⑨ INTEREST EXPENSE	(7,572)	.02	+ 227%	(5,966)	.01	- 21%
⑩ OTHER INCOME/EXPENSE (NET)	(7)	-	-	3,110	.01	N.C.
⑪ PRETAX INCOME (LOSS)	(11,580)	.03	- 155%	51,571	.10	+ 545%
⑫ INCOME TAXES (+/-)	4,111	.01	N.C.	(16,504)	.04	N.C.
⑬ NET INCOME (LOSS)	(7,469)	.02	- 150%	35,067	.06	+ 570%

(AMOUNTS IN THOUSANDS)

EXHIBIT 9.4 Coded Statements of Income for Spreadsheet Analysis—The ABC Corporation

Years ended December 31 (in thousands, except per-share amounts)

		1991	1990	1989
Net sales	①	$533,814	$456,520	$412,721
Cost of sales	②	360,439	344,334	295,803
Gross profit		173,375	112,186	116,918
Selling and marketing expenses	④	71,596	66,354	55,538
General and administrative expenses	⑤	28,911	32,889	22,705
Research and development expenses	⑥	18,441	16,944	15,693
Total operating expenses		118,948	116,187	93,936
Operating income (loss)		54,427	(4,001)	22,982
Interest income	⑩	4,804	1,490	950
Interest expense	⑨	(5,966)	(7,572)	(2,314)
Other expense, net	⑩	(1,694)	(1,497)	(686)
Income (loss) before provision (benefit) for income taxes		51,571	(11,580)	20,932
Provision (benefit) for income taxes	⑫	16,504	(4,111)	5,861
Net income (loss)		$ 35,067	$ (7,469)	$ 15,071
Net income (loss) per share		2.86	(0.64)	1.28
Weighted average common shares outstanding		12,265	11,580	11,743

The accompanying notes are an integral part of the financial statements.

17 percent, and most of this increase was due to volume. Operating expenses are up only 2 percent. Were they too high in the first place? This is easy enough to check. Research the company's recent historical past and make some industry comparisons using the spreadsheet technique. The more you work with this tool, the more adept you will become in determining a company's financial condition and performance as represented by its balance sheet and income statement positions.

Our next stop in this journey through the financial section of an annual report takes us to Chapter 10 and a review of the statement of cash flows.

10

THE INFLOWS AND OUTFLOWS OF CASH

☐ THE STATEMENT OF CASH FLOWS

What is cash flow? Paul J. Hoeper, a financial consultant writing in the April, 1991, issue of the *AAII Journal*, provided one of the best, easy-to-understand descriptions: "Cash inflows and outflows are the heart-beat of a business. The cash flow statement tells how a company spends its money and where that money comes from. The cash flow statement is much like a summary of a firm's checking account." You will, nevertheless, encounter several definitions of cash flow depending on the context of the usage and who is using it. In the context of an annual report presentation, Hoeper's definition fits perfectly.

The statement of cash flows categorizes a company's cash receipts and disbursements by three major activities: operations, investing and financing. The results of a year's activities are reconciled with the year's beginning cash balance to provide a year-end cash figure. Exhibit 10.1 shows ABC's "Cash and cash investments at end of year" for 1991 registering $92,252,000, which is precisely the figure carried in its "Cash and cash equivalents" account in its 1991 balance sheet. If you believe in the old adage that "it takes money to make money," then you have grasped the essence of cash flow. The experts know that cash flow is a better indicator of a company's operating performance

EXHIBIT 10.1 Consolidated Statements of Cash Flows—The ABC Corporation

Years ended December 31 (in thousands)	1991	1990	1989
Cash flows from operating activities:			
Net income (loss)	$35,067	$ (7,469)	$ 15,071
Adjustments to reconcile net income (loss) to net cash provided by (used in) operating activities:			
Depreciation and amortization	11,313	11,349	6,382
Provision for deferred taxes	1,881	2,655	(1,131)
Decrease (increase) in accounts receivable	(4,557)	6,702	(48,734)
Decrease (increase) in inventories	18,188	39,275	(73,180)
Decrease (increase) in prepaid expenses	10,621	(11,921)	–
Decrease (increase) in other current assets	(843)	(18)	437
Increase (decrease) in accounts payable and accrued liabilities	14,365	(25,523)	42,251
Increase in other current liabilities	5,016	401	349
Exchange (gain) loss	(556)	1,924	399
Net cash provided by (used in) operating activities	90,495	17,375	(58,156)
Cash flows from investing activities:			
Capital expenditures	(11,148)	(11,840)	(14,568)
Acquisition of subsidiaries, net of cash acquired	–	(2,243)	–
Acquisition of other assets	(1,576)	(1,231)	(2,369)
Net cash used in investing activities	(12,724)	(15,314)	(16,937)
Cash flows from financing activities:			
Short-term borrowings (repayments)	704	(4,500)	4,500
Net proceeds (repayments) of long-term debt	(5,119)	(422)	50,663
Proceeds from issuance of common stock	2,688	1,030	559
Net cash provided by (used in) financing activities	(1,727)	(3,892)	55,722
Effect of exchange rate changes on cash	(2,274)	(82)	(244)
Net increase (decrease) in cash	73,770	(1,913)	(19,371)
Cash and cash investments at beginning of year	18,482	20,395	39,766
Cash and cash investments at end of year	$ 92,252	$ 18,482	$ 20,395

The accompanying notes are an integral part of the financial statements.

than earnings. And adequate cash flow is the single most important element to a company's survival. Because of the level of importance of cash flow, you should have a solid understanding of how the cash flow statement works.

□ TWO FORMATS BUT THE SAME INFORMATION

Since 1988, the Financial Accounting Standards Board (FASB) has required companies to drop the statement of changes in financial position and replace it with one of two formats, the indirect or direct method, for a statement of cash flows. ABC's cash flow statement in Exhibit 10.1 represents the use of the indirect method. This approach determines cash flow by starting with net income and then providing for a series of adjustments to account for noncash charges in the income statement, e.g., depreciation, and changes in operating working capital to arrive at a net operating cash flow number. The direct method, which is used only by about one in ten companies, simply lists cash disbursements and cash receipts to arrive at the same net operating cash flow number. The only difference in the two methods is in the presentation of the operating cash flow section; otherwise, the statements are exactly alike. You can refer to Exhibit 10.2, which illustrates how ABC's operating cash flow section would appear under the direct method. The important thing to remember is not to be dismayed or confused by the 10 percent odds of encountering a direct format presentation. It may be somewhat unfamiliar, but the key number you need to work with, operating cash flow, is clearly indicated.

□ THE STRUCTURE OF THE CASH FLOW STATEMENT

As referred to previously, ABC's cash flow statement has three distinct sections, each of which describe the company's cash flow according to three separate corporate activities.

Cash Flow from Operations

Operating cash flow is the first and foremost source of a company's cash. If it is not, the company is definitely in trouble. These are internally generated funds from a company's operating activities. Quite obviously, the whole numbers represent inflows and those in

EXHIBIT 10.2 Operating Cash Flow—Direct Method—
The ABC Corporation

Years ended December 31 (in thousands)	1991	1990	1989
Cash flows from operating activities			
Cash received from customers	$527,030	$468,867	$363,378
Cash paid to suppliers and employees	(433,877)	(441,296)	(414,128)
Interest received	4,399	1,396	1,225
Interest paid, net of amounts capitalized	(6,545)	(7,312)	(1,939)
Income tax refund received	11,056	–	–
Income taxes paid	(10,361)	(5,251)	(7,005)
Other cash received (paid)	(1,207)	971	313
Net cash provided by (used in) operating activities	$ 90,495	$ 17,375	($58,156)

brackets outflows. As you can see in ABC's statement, net income and depreciation are major sources of operating cash flow. For many financial commentators and investment information/advisory services, the sum of these two items represents *cash flow*. While they are important components of cash flow, such a narrow definition can lead to faulty judgments.

The operating working capital items in current assets and liabilities, sometimes expressed as a net subtotal, are important elements in determining operating cash flow. Some annual report presentations include an operating working capital reconciliation in the actual cash flow statement, others provide the information in a note and most, unfortunately, leave this calculation to the reader's imagination. Exhibit 10.3 shows how the net increase/decrease in operating working capital would appear for ABC. These are key numbers. You learned in Chapter 7 that a growing company can generate a positive working capital balance, but if the company is not converting its receivables and inventory into cash, a company's liquidity will suffer.

It is worth clarifying again that, contrary to conventional wisdom, it is *not* good for a company to tie up a lot of money in working capital. This point is well illustrated by contrasting ABC's 1989 and 1991 operating working capital results. The reconciliation in Exhibit 10.3 shows that the growth of operating current assets, basically receivables and inventory, in 1989 required $121,914,000 in cash. Liabilities did not grow correspondingly, resulting in a $78,877,000 increase in the use of funds by operating working capital. Contrast this circum-

EXHIBIT 10.3 Reconciliation of Operating Working Capital—
The ABC Corporation

Years ended December 31 (in thousands)	1991	1990	1989
Decrease (increase) in accounts receivable	$(4,557)	$ 6,702	$(48,734)
Decrease (increase) in inventories	18,188	39,275	(73,180)
Decrease (increase) in prepaid expenses	10,621	(11,291)	–
Decrease (increase) in other current assets	(843)	(18)	437
Increase (decrease) in accounts payable and accrued liabilities	14,365	(25,523)	42,251
Increase (decrease) in other current liabilities	5,016	401	349
Net decrease (increase) in operating working capital	$42,790	$ 8,916	$(78,877)

stance to 1991 when operating working capital *provided* (or decreased the use of) $42,790,000 in cash.

The purpose of reviewing the behavior of operating working capital, as reflected in the cash flow statement, is to highlight its impact on cash and management's reactions. Finally, the greater the surplus of cash from operations, the more funds a company has to cover essential outlays, to avoid borrowing, to expand or to withstand hard times. A stable, positive operating cash flow is a good indicator of a healthy company.

Cash Flow from Investing

Generally, this activity will be a user of cash. This category includes such items as capital expenditures on property, plant and equipment and their disposition; the acquisition and sale of investments in affiliates; and the buying/selling of short-term invested funds. The key number in investment cash flow is that for capital expenditures. It generally is assumed that this use of cash is necessary for the proper maintenance of and the additions to a company's physical plant to support its operations at an adequate level. In ABC's case, its investing cash flow activities are focused essentially on spending for capital improvements. Typically, cash flows from investing activities represent a use of funds.

Cash Flow from Financing

A company's financing activities can involve a combination of debt and equity proceeds and repayments representing both cash inflows and cash outflows. ABC's financing cash flows are, accordingly, representative of this circumstance. The company did not pay a dividend, however, so that entry, as a cash outflow, does not appear in its statement. High growth companies such as ABC cannot afford to pay dividends; instead they prefer to keep their earnings in their companies to facilitate additional growth. It is important, particularly for investors, however, to understand that dividends are paid from cash. The payment of cash dividends obviously not only requires profits but also sufficient cash availabilities.

The net effect of a company's operating, investing and financing activities appears on the line "Net increase (decrease) in cash" near the bottom of the statement. Applying the simplistic analytical rule of more of a good thing is better, it is fairly easy to conclude that cash increases are the preferred result. You should recognize, however, that events of a nonrecurring nature (significant acquisition activity, large debt proceeds or repayments and equity injections) will affect this number. Reiterating my previous remarks, it is the operating cash flow number that should reflect stability and consistent growth for a company that is expanding its operations. The remaining lines in the cash flow statement simply reconcile the beginning and ending cash and cash investment amounts, also expressed in the balance sheet, for the year in question. As you can see, ABC will begin its 1992 fiscal year with a substantial amount of cash! Let us now discuss some of the commonly applied measurements of cash adequacy to the elements we have highlighted in the cash flow statement.

☐ CASH FLOW RATIOS AND INDICATORS

It is regrettable but true that most annual report presentations include little in the way of supplemental cash flow information. Other than the cash flow statement itself and some cursory, generalized commentary in the MD&A section, there is not much analytical focus on a company's cash flow. There are exceptions, of course. To compensate for this absence of ratios, indicators and insightful commentary, I will provide some helpful techniques that you can easily apply to aid in your analysis of the cash flow statement.

There is increasing use in the financial press and investment advisory material of the term *free cash flow*. As far as I know, there is, as yet, no universal definition of this concept. You will be safe in using one of these two versions:

Free cash flow = Operating cash flow − Capital expenditures

or

= Operating cash flow − (Capital expenditures + Cash dividends)

You can assume that free cash flow is good, so you can guess what this implies—more of it is better. It seems to me that the former definition is used more than the latter. Whatever the calculation, these comparisons can be revealing. With all due respect to free cash flow, whatever it is, I suggest that you make four easily computed comparisons to operating cash flow that include the free cash flow perspective.

First, a comparison of operating cash flow to capital expenditures indicates the coverage that internally generated funds provide for this generally considered mandatory cash outlay for property, plant and equipment. The larger the margin in the ratio, the less dependence there is on borrowing to finance these purchases and the more money there is left over to pay cash dividends. For the sake of simplicity, we will use ABC's 1990 and 1991 figures to illustrate this and the other ratios that follow:

	1990	1991
Operating cash flow:	$17,375	$90,495
Capital expenditures:	$11,840	$11,148
Cash flow coverage:	147%	812%

Needless to say, ABC had ample margin in both years to pay for its purchases of needed capital goods.

Second, a comparison of operating cash flow to the sum of capital expenditures and cash dividends applies a more stringent measurement of cash flow adequacy. To calculate this effect, let us assume that ABC paid a modest cash dividend in these years.

	1990	1991
Operating cash flow:	$17,375	$90,495
Capital expenditures:	$11,840	$11,148
Cash dividends paid:	$ 1,000	$ 2,000
Cash requirements:	$12,840	$13,148
Cash flow coverage:	135%	688%

There was still plenty of cash for ABC to cover these outlays. In fact, the board of directors probably gave serious consideration to declaring a special dividend in 1991.

Third, at this stage we add debt payments to the accumulating total of cash requirements. Generally, the figure for debt is the same one used for fixed charges (interest expense + current portion of long-term debt), which was covered in the discussion of earnings-related ratios in the preceding chapter.

	1990	1991
Operating cash flow:	$17,375	$90,495
Capital expenditures:	$11,840	$11,148
Cash dividends paid:	$ 1,000	$ 2,000
Fixed charges:	$ 8,285	$ 6,702
Cash requirements:	$21,125	$19,850
Cash flow coverage:	82%	456%

In addition to some new equity funds, ABC had to tap some of its accumulated cash from the year before to cover its cash needs in 1990. Obviously, 1991 was a good year for cash flow.

This type of cash flow statement analysis demonstrates a company's ability to meet a hierarchy of cash requirements from net operating cash flow. While there is nothing inherently wrong with debt and equity financing, access to these sources of funds is not always readily available. The bigger the contribution of operating cash flow to a company's cash needs, the better.

One last comment about cash flow. While all annual reports provide the earnings per-share figure, you will have to calculate your own cash flow per-share number. For ABC in 1991, this would involve: net operating cash flow ($90,495,000) ÷ the average number of shares outstanding (approximately 13,441,515 shares) = a cash flow per share of $6.73. Many financial commentators view this indicator as more valuable than earnings per share because of the latter's potential for manipulation by the selection of accounting policies and tax actions.

11 THE EQUITY BASE

□ THE STATEMENT OF SHAREHOLDERS' EQUITY

For those of you who relished those unexpected free periods in school when something happened to cancel the scheduled class, as I did, you are about to repeat that wonderful experience. Remember the feeling? The pressure was off and you could just relax, do nothing, or next to nothing, for a brief period of time in an otherwise educationally stressful day. This chapter, or rather the subject matter of this chapter, is the equivalent of one of those "free periods"!

□ NOT MUCH TO CONCERN YOURSELF WITH

The strict rules applied to the preparation of an investment prospectus dictate that when the configuration of the document results in a page with nothing on it, the reader is advised in a notation: "This page intentionally left blank." I gave serious consideration to adopting this technique to this chapter. Even though the statement of shareholders' equity may occupy a full page with numerous account entries and number-filled columns, it receives little or no attention from analysts or writers of financial analysis material. There is good reason for this. You do not have to read or understand anything about this particular financial statement.

In terms of its practical relevance to analyzing a company's financial position, the shareholders' equity statement definitely falls into the nice-to-know rather than the need-to-know category. Books and articles on financial statement analysis hardly mention, if at all, the equity statement. Therefore, when encountering a statement of shareholders' equity during the perusal of a company's annual report, enjoy one of those scholastic "free periods" of yesteryears!

☐ RECONCILING THE OWNERS' INVESTMENT

Just for the record, however, you should know that a statement of shareholders' equity simply provides a reconciliation of the changes in the various components of a company's equity position over the three-year period being reviewed in the annual report. Exhibit 11.1, presenting the ABC Corporation's equity statement, is fairly uncomplicated and representative of what you will encounter in most annual report presentations. For what it is worth, you will note that the amounts for common stock, additional paid-in capital and retained earnings match those found in the shareholders' equity section of ABC's balance sheet illustrated in Exhibit 7.1 on page 43. In some instances, this information appears as part of the notes to the financial statements. If this approach is used, the data on the retained earnings component may be added on to the income statement or presented in a separate statement of retained earnings.

Other than these observations, there is little more to concern yourself with regarding the statement of shareholders' equity. In contrast to this position, the subject matter of the next chapter, the notes to the financial statements, is probably one of the most important financial reporting elements for you to understand and use when analyzing the financial position of a company.

EXHIBIT 11.1 Consolidated Statements of Shareholders' Equity—The ABC Corporation

| (in thousands) | Common Stock | | Additional Paid-In Capital | Retained Earnings |
	Shares	Amount		
Balance at December 31, 1988	11,405	$ 32,599	$ –	$ 66,547
Reincorporation in Delaware	–	(32,485)	32,485	–
Exercise of stock options	65	1	559	–
Tax benefit related to employee stock options	–	–	142	–
Net income	–	–	–	15,071
Balance at December 31, 1989	11,470	115	33,186	81,618
Exercise of stock options	158	2	1,028	–
Tax benefit related to employee stock options	–	–	319	–
Net loss	–	–	–	(7,469)
Balance at December 31, 1990	11,628	117	34,533	74,149
Exercise of stock options	299	3	2,333	–
Tax benefit related to employee stock options	–	–	879	–
Issuance of restricted stock	263	2	350	–
Conversion of subordinated debentures, net of conversion cost	3,065	31	45,822	–
Net income				
Balance at December 31, 1991	15,255	$ 153	$ 83,917	$109,216

The accompanying notes are an integral part of the financial statements.

12

READING THE FINE PRINT

☐ NOTES TO FINANCIAL STATEMENTS

What is so important about the notes to a company's financial statements? You have seen numerous references to this chapter in this book. The financial statements in an annual report all carry a notation suggesting that you refer to these notes. So there must be something of value here. There is, and it is extremely valuable!

It is difficult for the numbers in the financials alone to provide the adequate financial disclosure required by the regulatory authorities. Also, financial accounting allows for estimates, judgments and the alternative application of accounting methods. The notes highlight and explain these management actions. Therefore, notes, often referred to as footnotes, provide the users of financial statements with additional, detailed information that helps them to properly evaluate a company's financials.

Unfortunately, many notes to financial statements sections in annual reports have a rather low readability factor. A lot of technical financial jargon appears to be crammed into a less-than-stimulating format. Often, the writing is somewhat incomprehensible to the less-experienced (financially) reader. Nevertheless, you must not be deterred. Many companies are making an effort to improve the note presentations in annual reports, and you do not have to understand all the content to obtain valuable insights to a company's financial condition and performance.

The diversity of companies and the varied nature of the contents of a notes section make it virtually impossible to cover all the potentially important items that could appear there. In view of this complexity, I am going to suggest that you focus your attention on seven fairly standard notes that generally include key informational inputs. This does not absolve you from completely reading the notes section, but it will at least give you the fundamentally important material. Here is another suggestion for dealing with the notes section. Use the glossary at the back of this book to help you with many of the terms that you may find hard to understand.

☐ ACCOUNTING POLICIES

These policies, which indicate what accounting methods the company employs to various aspects of its operations, must be enumerated in an annual report. They will appear either as the first note in the notes to financial statements or as a separate section just prior to the presentation of the notes section. They generally are called "Summary of Significant Accounting Policies" and will cover such items, among others, as consolidation, inventory, depreciation, income and expense recognition, intangible assets, pensions, stock plans and income taxes.

You should look for three things that may be important. First, be aware of any changes in these policies and their impact on a company's financial position and performance. For example, a change in the estimated useful life of a significant fixed asset or group of fixed assets would affect depreciation charges and have an impact on earnings. Such consequences are described in this note and/or in a subsequent note. The accounting policies note tends to look like boilerplate text, but you need to know what these policies are and the consequences of changes. I highly recommend Thorton L. O'glove's book, *The Quality of Earnings*, for its perspective on the influence of accounting changes on a company's profitability. As O'glove states, "Accountants know quite well and the general public, including investors, hardly at all, that according to the methods used, a company can report a very wide range of earnings."

Second, the degree of conservatism in the presentation of a company's earnings depends, basically, on two accounting policies: the inventory valuation method and the depreciation method. As discussed in Chapter 9, the LIFO inventory method is more conservative than the

FIFO inventory method. Accelerated depreciation is more conservative than the straight-line method. However, I have yet to see accelerated depreciation applied to financial statement accounting in an annual report.

Third, some companies use accounting policies that run counter to general practice but conform to industry practice. For example, tobacco and alcoholic beverage companies classify leaf tobacco and bulk whiskey inventories as current assets. In reality, these products will not be sold and converted to cash for several years. It is an industry practice, however, to classify these items as current in their companies' balance sheets.

□ ACQUISITIONS

The note on acquisitions, which is fairly self-explanatory, mentions either the purchase method or the pooling of interests method as the basis for the business combination in question. The former method is the one most often used. With this approach, the acquired company becomes a part of the consolidated operations of the parent company as of the date of purchase. The purchase price frequently exceeds the market value of the acquired company's net asset value. This creates an intangible asset, goodwill or purchased goodwill, in the parent company's balance sheet.

The pooling of interests method, which requires conformity to a long list of conditions, unites two companies through an exchange of stock. Their recorded assets and liabilities are fused together in a new combined corporation. Earnings for the full year are attributed to the new entity regardless of the purchase date, which tends to inflate the surviving entity's true profit performance. In addition, any subsequent disposition of the acquired company's assets can produce aberrations in profit reporting in later years.

□ DEBT AND BORROWING ARRANGEMENTS

Debt is an important financial consideration for any company, so it follows logically that the note on debt and borrowing arrangements is important to read and understand. Exhibit 12.1 illustrates the debt note from McCormick & Company's 1991 annual report. This is a good example of an informative note for it discloses the general nature and amount of the company's committed and uncommitted lines of credit

EXHIBIT 12.1 Note on Debt and Borrowing Arrangements—McCormick & Company, 1991

---

3. Financing Arrangements and Long-Term Debt:

At November 30, 1991, the Company had available credit facilities with domestic and foreign banks in the aggregate of $236,000. The Company maintains these credit facilities largely to assure liquidity and support commercial paper issuance. There were no borrowings outstanding against these facilities at November 30, 1991. The Company is required to pay a commitment fee on the unused portion of these facilities.

The Company has short-term lending arrangements for the benefit of its foreign subsidiaries which provide for lines of credit aggregating $31,500. Borrowings under these agreements totaled $4,120 at November 30, 1991. The Company also has informal money market rate borrowing agreements with its domestic and foreign banks in excess of $300,000, subject to availability of funds; compensation is not required. Short-term borrowings under these arrangements totaled $19,300 at November 30, 1991.

At November 30, 1991, the Company had unconditionally guaranteed the debt of affiliates amounting to $1,925.

The Company's long-term debt at November 30 consisted of the following:

	1991	1990
8.95% note due July 2001	**$ 74,157**	$ —
9.00% installment note due March 2002	**22,727**	25,000
9.75% installment note due April 2003	**35,000**	35,000
11.68% non-recourse installment note due December 2006	**61,764**	63,283
Variable rate notes	**—**	38,590
8.30% note due December 1991	**—**	30,000
Industrial revenue bonds	**10,034**	16,154
Other	**3,945**	3,440
Total	**$207,627**	$211,467

The installment note agreements require sinking fund payments. The Company's long-term debt agreements contain various restrictive covenants including payment of cash dividends. Under the most restrictive covenant, $212,131 of retained earnings was available for dividends at November 30, 1991.

Industrial revenue bonds are payable in installments from 1992 to 2002 with interest rates ranging from 4.35% to 7.63%.

The non-recourse installment note is secured by property and equipment owned by Gilroy Energy Company, Inc. with a net book value of $73,340.

Included in other long-term debt are capital lease obligations aggregating $658 due in installments to 1997.

Maturities of long-term debt during the four years subsequent to November 30, 1992 are as follows:

1993 – $7,329	1995 – $10,193
1994 – $8,467	1996 – $ 8,602

The Company enters into forward exchange contracts to hedge the impact of foreign currency fluctuations on its net investments in certain foreign subsidiaries. At November 30, 1991, the Company had outstanding $39,131 of forward exchange contracts with commercial banks expiring in 1992. The gains or losses on these contracts are included in the foreign currency translation adjustments account within shareholders' equity.

Interest paid in 1991, 1990 and 1989 was $25,233; $29,399 and $30,659 respectively, of which $741 and $268 was capitalized in 1991 and 1990 respectively.

Source: McCormick & Company 1991 Annual Report

with its banks. I would like to see the principal institutions named, but that practice is a rarity. Guarantees of other debt are mentioned, which in this case involves affiliates. The note details the company's long-term debt.

Take notice of the amounts subject to fixed rates versus variable rates. The future behavior of the company's interest expense account could be influenced by this structure. Restrictive covenants are mentioned, but as is the case with McCormick, few details generally are provided. *Covenants,* both positive and negative, are conditions placed in a credit agreement by a creditor to protect its position as a lender. Here again, I would like to see more specific details, particularly if a company is highly indebted or is in a problematical debt situation. Other data provided include debt maturities, interest paid and the amount of capitalized interest.

Two items not appearing in the McCormick note are worth mentioning. A *shelf-registration* is a liquidity enhancement for a company. In this case, the SEC has given prior approval to a company for the issuance of debt or equity securities. The company then can react quickly to unexpected needs or favorable market conditions to raise funds. Finally, corporate bond issues are subject to ratings by agencies such as Moody's, Standard & Poor's, Fitch and Duff & Phelps. These ratings are sometimes mentioned in the debt note or in the MD&A section of an annual report. Corporate management is sensitive to these ratings and for good reason. A downgrading of a rating can cost a company a considerable amount of money in interest expense, as well as create problems with creditors. Conversely, an upgrading can make it easier to borrow and at better rates.

□ OPERATING LEASE COMMITMENTS

Generally, operating leases represent multiyear, noncancellable obligations for the use of assets. As discussed in Chapter 8, these are debtlike obligations that most analysts consider as *off-balance-sheet* debt financing. Exhibit 12.2 illustrates a typical lease commitments note that contains operating and capital lease information. In the case of capital leases, the *net present value* amount will be incorporated as part of the company's long-term debt obligations. The operating lease amount, however, is treated differently. It is mentioned in a note but does not become part of a company's balance sheet. In the case of CIS Technologies, the $1.6 million in operating leases represents more than 50 percent of its net fixed assets of $3.1 million and exceeds its total long-term liabilities of $1.3 million. The point is that it is not an

EXHIBIT 12.2 Note on Lease Commitments—Nordson Corporation, 1991

The Company has lease commitments expiring at various dates, principally for warehouse and office space, automobiles and office equipment. Most leases contain renewal options and some contain purchase options.

During 1990, the Company entered into an operating lease for office space from a partnership in which the Company is a partner. The lease is for 20 years with an option to purchase the property at fair market value after 10 years. Monthly payments, which began in December 1991, range from $73,000 to $108,000 and approximate market rates.

Rent expense for all operating leases was approximately $5,349,000 in 1991 ($3,755,000 in 1990 and $3,408,000 in 1989).

Assets held under capitalized leases are included in property, plant and equipment as follows:

	1991	1990
	(In thousands)	
Transportation equipment	$8,314	$7,707
Other	1,084	929
Total capitalized leases	9,398	8,636
Less accumulated amortization	3,602	3,239
Net capitalized leases	$5,796	$5,397

At November 3, 1991, future minimum lease payments under noncancellable capitalized and operating leases are as follows:

	Capitalized Leases	Operating Leases
	(In thousands)	
Fiscal Year Ending:		
1992	$3,246	$ 4,902
1993	2,532	3,338
1994	1,511	2,518
1995	324	2,107
1996	23	1,496
Later years	—	17,617
Total minimum lease payments	7,636	$31,978
Less amount representing executory costs	827	
Net minimum lease payments	6,809	
Less amount representing interest	1,013	
Present value of net minimum lease payments	5,796	
Less current portion	2,437	
Long-term obligations at November 3, 1991	$3,359	

Source: Nordson Corporation 1991 Annual Report

insignificant amount in the overall context of the company's financial position. Depending on the degree of conservatism you are comfortable with, either two-thirds, or perhaps the whole amount, of operating leases should figure into your debt measurement calculations as principal.

□ PENSION AND RETIREMENT BENEFITS

The importance of the note on pension and retirement benefits cannot be overestimated. David R. Vruwink, associate professor of accounting at Kansas State University, Manhattan, Kansas, in the September, 1990, issue of *Business Credit*, provides ample evidence to support this view: "The largest category of corporate debt for U.S. companies is neither bonds nor bank debt, but pension benefits that companies owe to their employees. U.S. companies owe their employees about $700 billion while about $500 billion each is owed to their bondholders and banks."

The requirement (by 1993) to record postretirement health-care benefits on an accrual basis, just like pension benefits, instead of on a pay-as-you-go basis, has increased this burden. According to some estimates, the cost of these benefits could reach as high as $1 trillion over the next few years for U.S. companies. Most young and financially strong companies are not expected to be hard hit by the new retiree health-care rule. Mature companies, however, especially those with marginal operations and/or with a large number of retirees, could be negatively impacted.

The pension note, the calculations of pension expense, the funding position of the plan and the actuarial assumptions are quite complex. Focus your attention on four fundamental aspects that will at least provide you with a basic overview of a company's pension and retirement benefits position. First, determine if the company is providing a defined benefit or a defined contribution plan. There is a subtle but important distinction between the two. The former approach makes it difficult (how much will the benefit cost in the future?) for a company to ascertain its liability obligation and, consequently, the future impact on its financial position. In contrast, the defined contribution approach (a specific dollar amount is predetermined) allows a company to exercise control over the extent of its liability and its subsequent financial impact.

Second, review the annual behavior of the *pension expense* amount. A table, which is fairly self explanatory, is presented within the note and provides this information. Accelerating increases may be cause for concern in the future.

Third, determine if a company's *plan assets at fair value* exceed its *projected benefit obligation*. There is a table reflecting this status that indicates the funding status of the pension plan or plans. Obviously, an underfunded status, depending on its magnitude, is cause for concern.

Fourth, compare the actuarial assumptions, also provided in a table or within the text of the note, to those of other companies in the industry. The *discount rate* is used to determine the present value of the projected benefit obligation. The *rate of return on assets* is an estimate of the expected long-term rate of return on the plan's assets (investments). The *rate of compensation increases*, as the term implies, is an estimate of the growth rate in salary costs. Management's selection of these rates obviously can affect the final outcome of its pension expense and liability. The only practical way that you can determine the reasonableness of these assumptions is to make intercompany comparisons on an industry basis.

☐ BUSINESS SEGMENT INFORMATION

Diversified businesses with multilines or products will provide a breakdown of these segments of the company by sales, operating profits, assets, depreciation and capital expenditures. In addition, if appropriate, this same information will be provided on a geographic basis. This segment information makes it possible to divide the whole company into its individual parts, which, as a consequence, allows you to evaluate the performance of each component. For example, using the business segment data of Worthington Industries illustrated in Exhibit 12.3, you will see three distinct divisions or product lines presented. A wealth of information is here if you take a little time to do some elemental number-crunching.

For instance, using the 1991 figures, we can conclude that processed steel products is the heavy hitter in Worthington's lineup. Its sales account for 70 percent of the company's total sales and its profit margin (pretax income ÷ sales) is 10.8 percent, down slightly from the 12 percent levels registered in 1988 and 1989, but way out in front of the 3.9 and 2.2 percent recorded by custom and cast products, respectively. It has the lion's share of assets and capital expenditures, which, along with its earnings, produces the bulk of the company's cash flow, as measured by segment data (pretax income plus depreciation). Its

EXHIBIT 12.3 Note on Business Segment Information—Worthington Industries, 1991

INDUSTRY SEGMENT DATA

Worthington Industries, Inc. and Subsidiaries

	In thousands May 31	1991	1990	1989	1988	1987
SALES	**Net Sales and Revenues**					
	Processed steel products	$613,691	$652,479	$658,575	$622,406	$540,547
	Custom products	186,508	165,351	182,085	155,113	143,989
	Cast products	74,685	98,083	98,587	63,886	81,634
		$874,884	$915,913	$939,247	$841,405	$766,170
EARNINGS	**Earnings From Continuing Operations Before Income Taxes**					
	Processed steel products	$ 65,942	$ 73,946	$ 77,806	$ 77,760	$ 65,474
	Custom products	7,192	7,838	15,889	12,276	14,295
	Cast products	1,642	10,075	10,784	605	2,498
	Interest expense	(4,807)	(4,245)	(4,404)	(3,888)	(4,064)
		$ 69,969	$ 87,614	$100,075	$ 86,753	$ 78,203
ASSETS	**Identifiable Assets**					
	Processed steel products	$366,097	$334,927	$318,357	$293,800	$245,702
	Custom products	94,820	91,121	78,386	66,764	53,220
	Cast products	65,311	59,560	56,370	44,875	47,386
	Corporate	37,617	75,008	65,587	59,804	73,736
	Continuing Operations	563,845	560,616	518,700	465,243	420,044
	Discontinued Operation	—	—	39,087	41,387	35,169
		$563,845	$560,616	$557,787	$506,630	$455,213
DEPRECIATION	**Depreciation Expense**					
	Processed steel products	$ 13,230	$ 10,983	$ 9,965	$ 8,533	$ 7,072
	Custom products	4,990	4,246	3,667	3,545	3,081
	Cast products	5,623	5,561	5,137	5,010	5,518
		$ 23,843	$ 20,790	$ 18,769	$ 17,088	$ 15,671
EXPENDITURES	**Capital Expenditures**					
	Processed steel products	$ 45,554	$ 33,561	$ 21,147	$ 18,743	$ 10,076
	Custom products	8,527	12,653	11,299	5,752	5,639
	Cast products	9,238	8,344	11,118	4,638	3,177
		$ 63,319	$ 54,558	$ 43,564	$ 29,133	$ 18,892

( ) Indicates deduction

Corporate expenses are allocated on a consistent basis among industry segments over the five-year period.
"Capital expenditures" are net of normal disposals and exclude amounts in connection with acquisitions and divestitures.

See notes to consolidated financial statements.

Source: Worthington Industries 1991 Annual Report

return on average assets is 18.8 percent, compared to 7.7 and 2.6 percent for the other product lines. There could be more to this analysis, but this brief look should give you an idea of how you can use business segment information.

Among other helpful insights, being able to distinguish the strong and weak performers in a company's product line is valuable. This is especially so if different industry sectors are involved. For the sake of this discussion, let us assume that a company's business segments sell into distinct markets. Obviously, an expansion of a low-margin market segment's business would contribute relatively little to the company's overall profitability. Growth rates in sales and earnings should also be compared. How do these results compare to the allocation of capital expenditures? Finally, tracking profit margins and the return on assets over five years, as the generous data provided by Worthington's presentation allows you to do, can be quite revealing.

□ COMMITMENTS AND CONTINGENCIES

Commitments differ materially from contingencies, although often they are discussed as one and the same. Commitments generally are quantifiable and represent proactive, positive positions of corporate management, e.g., proposed capital expenditures for the expansion of operating facilities. *Contingencies*, on the other hand, are much more uncertain in their ultimate consequences and, if they do occur, tend to adversely affect the company. The most common of these potential liabilities relate to litigation and guarantees.

A standard phrase in the contingency note states that the circumstance in question "will, in the opinion of management, result in no material loss to the company," or words to that effect. Hopefully, that is always the case. You should read this note carefully, however, and use your common sense. Environmental liability is a particularly sensitive area with some potentially large risks. As a rule of thumb, the longer and more complicated a note, the more likely that the contingency is a serious one. Often it is difficult to quantify a given contingent risk, and while it may appear to be self-serving, companies are reluctant to make estimates without full and complete information on the risk. In the end, on issues such as these, by the time you read about them in the annual report, it probably is too late to provide any warning.

13

WHAT DO THE AUDITORS SAY?

☐ THE AUDITORS' AND MANAGEMENT REPORTS

The auditors' report and, when presented, the report of management usually are found at the beginning or at the end of an annual report's presentation of a company's financial information. Publicly held companies are required by the SEC to provide audited financial statements, so you always will find the reports of the auditing firms that conducted the independent audits in the annual reports of such companies. It is absolutely essential that you read these reports first. On the other hand, the management statements of responsibility for the companies' financial statements are pretty much cases of standardized boilerplate text of little consequence.

☐ THE REPORT OF MANAGEMENT: NONESSENTIAL READING

This formalized statement (see Exhibit 13.1) is still an optional feature in financial reporting, but its appearance in annual reports is becoming more commonplace. A nice feature of this item is that you do *not* need to read it! If it does not appear, do not be overly concerned. Why? For appearances' sake, companies should provide such statements; however, these statements simply confirm, in print, what most of us assume is the case without having to read about it. That is to say, that management is responsible for:

EXHIBIT 13.1 Report of Management

MANAGEMENT'S RESPONSIBILITY FOR FINANCIAL STATEMENTS

Management is responsible for the company's financials. This also is expressed in the auditors' report.

Management is responsible for the fairness, integrity and objectivity of the company's financial statements, including all related information presented in this Annual Report. These statements have been prepared in accordance with generally accepted accounting principles and include amounts based on management's best estimates and judgments.

Management is responsible for reliable internal controls regarding accounting records.

Management maintains and relies on a system of internal controls that provides reasonable assurance that assets are safeguarded and transactions are properly recorded. The system includes written policies and procedures and an organizational structure that provides for segregation of responsibilities and the selection and training of qualified personnel. In addition, the Company has an internal audit function that evaluates existing controls and recommends changes and improvements deemed necessary.

Usually comprised of independent, outside directors for this oversight responsibility.

The *Audit Committee of the Board of Directors,* which is comprised of two nonmanagement directors, meets periodically with senior financial officers, independent accountants and internal auditors. They discuss significant financial transactions and the scope and major findings of the independent accountants' and internal auditors' audits and review the adequacy of the system of internal controls.

Management affirms the reliability of the company's financials.

Management believes that the company's policies and procedures, as well as its internal control system and the activities of the internal and independent auditors and the Audit Committee, provide you, the shareholder, *with reasonable assurance as to the integrity of the financial statements.*

I. M. Strait
Chairman of the Board and
Chief Executive Officer

- The preparation, fairness and integrity of a company's financial statements;

- The maintenance of a system of internal accounting controls; and

- The establishment of an independent audit committee of the board of directors that provides oversight in the areas of financial reporting and controls.

Also, management's responsibility for a company's financials is stated clearly in the introductory paragraph of the auditors' report. The content of the report by management may vary somewhat from company to company, but in essence, the message, as indicated previously, is basically the same.

☐ THE AUDITORS' REPORT: ESSENTIAL READING

The report of a company's outside auditors is a totally different story in terms of its importance, meaning and relevance to users of annual report financial statement information. As mentioned in Chapter 1, the auditors' report is the *first* item to look at in a company's annual report. Before going into the details of why this is so, take time here to read the definitions provided in the glossary for *auditors, audit, audited statements* and *generally accepted accounting principles* (GAAP).

Financial statements provide essential information about a company's financial position and performance. Because the preparation and presentation of this information is the responsibility of management, an audit lends credibility to a company's financial statements. When a company's financials are accompanied by an auditors' standard audit report, you can be reasonably sure that management's accounting representations and the numbers in the financials are reliable. It is equally important, however, to understand what an auditors' report does not represent. It is *not:*

1. An endorsement of a company's financial position,

2. A 100 percent guarantee against material misstatement or

3. Any indication that the company is a good investment or financially sound.

Let us take a look at the new three-paragraph standard report (see Exhibit 13.2) that the accounting profession adopted in 1989. The words and phrases in the introductory, scope and opinion paragraphs have been chosen carefully to communicate the auditors' responsibility to financial statement users.

EXHIBIT 13.2 The Standard Auditors' Report Format

Introductory Paragraph

Evidence of audited financials.

Definition of management's and auditors' responsibilities.

Scope Paragraph

Compliance with professional standards.

Not an absolute guarantee!

Audit results provide a basis for an opinion.

Opinion Paragraph

Auditors' professional judgment.

Concept of fair presentation.

Financials are consistent with GAAP.

REPORT OF INDEPENDENT ACCOUNTANTS

To the Shareholders and Board of Directors of the ZYX Company:

We have *audited* the accompanying consolidated balance sheet of ZYX Company and Subsidiaries as of December 31, 1990, and 1991, and the related consolidated statements of income, shareholders' equity and cash flows for the years ended December 31, 1989, 1990 and 1991. *These financial statements are the responsibility of the Company's management. Our responsibility is to express an opinion on these financial statements based on our audits.*

We conducted our audits *in accordance with generally accepted auditing standards.* Those standards require that we plan and perform the audit *to obtain reasonable assurance about whether the financial statements are free of material misstatement.* An audit includes examining, on a test basis, evidence supporting the amounts and disclosures in the financial statements. An audit also includes assessing the accounting principles used and significant estimates made by management, as well as evaluating the overall financial statement presentation. *We believe that our audits provide a reasonable basis for our opinion.*

In our opinion, the financial statements referred to above *present fairly, in all material respects,* the consolidated financial position of ZYX Company and Subsidiaries at December 31, 1990, and 1991, and the consolidated results of their operations and their cash flows for the years ended December 31, 1989, 1990 and 1991, *in conformity with generally accepted accounting principles.*

Goode, Onest & Korect
Hometown, USA
February 22, 1992

According to the study of corporate financial reporting by the American Institute of Certified Public Accountants (AICPA), *Accounting Trends and Techniques*, the vast majority of the respondents in the AICPA annual 600-company survey generally obtain a standard report just like the one illustrated here. What about the other companies; what kind of reports do they get? Any modification of or addition to the wording in a *standard report* is by definition a *nonstandard report*. Before explaining the various circumstances that require auditors to issue nonstandard reports, first a word of explanation regarding the new structure of the auditors' report, a term that now refers to the entire communication, i.e., all three paragraphs. The *auditors' opinion*, which in the old days often was used interchangeably with *auditors' report*, now refers only to the third paragraph of the new auditors' report. This apparently trivial distinction is important.

In previous financial parlance, if a company was given a clean bill of health by the auditors, their report was considered an *unqualified* (in accounting jargon, *without any impairing qualifying remarks*) or *clean* opinion. If there was a problem, the auditors' report contained qualifying language such as *subject to* (the resolution of a problematical circumstance). This was considered a qualified (in accounting jargon, *with impairing qualifying remarks*) opinion and readily alerted the reader to a potential financial uncertainty or danger. It was easy to spot the warning signals. Under the accounting profession's new opinion structure, the explicit *subject to* qualifying language has been dropped, and the auditors now simply disclose a company's problem(s) in the body of their report.

In brief, this means that you have to read the auditors' report more carefully. As you will see in the following section of this chapter, the auditors may issue a technically *unqualified opinion* (paragraph three is written in standard language) but add modifying language in a fourth paragraph. Because of this nonstandard report form, you must read the additional remarks carefully to assess their impact on the company's financials. Thus, my advice, as previously stated, is to *read the auditors' report before anything else in an annual report*. If it is in the standard report form, it will take you less than 60 seconds, and you can move on to more serious reading and number-crunching with a high degree of confidence. Nonstandard presentations mandate further scrutiny.

□ NONSTANDARD AUDITORS' REPORTS

The following explanations of nonstandard wording in an auditors' report and their particular relevance to the annual report user have been adapted from the AICPA's excellent guide for financial statement users, *Understanding Audits and the Auditors' Report*. This 40-page booklet is a comprehensive, clearly written piece on the subject and can be obtained from the AICPA's Publications Department, 1211 Avenue of the Americas, New York, NY 10036-8775.

Some of the more common circumstances that necessitate the use of nonstandard, explanatory language include the following.

Referring to the Report of Another Auditor

This circumstance occurs when a *material* portion of the audit work is performed by another auditor, e.g., when another firm of public accountants performs the audit of a subsidiary company or when previous years were audited by another firm. Specific information about the shared responsibility will appear in the introductory paragraph and reference to *the report of other auditors* will appear in the scope and opinion paragraphs.

Generally speaking, this nonstandard language should not be a major concern, i.e., it is a rather benign qualifying remark. In an era of global business expansion, it is not always possible for a CPA firm to reach every corner of the earth. You will notice, however, that the *other* auditor always remains anonymous. Apparently, the auditing profession is not disposed to give any exposure to its competitors. Who is this *other* auditor? If this firm's shared responsibility is material, I would feel a lot better if it were a recognized, respected firm as opposed to some outfit called "Dunce, Bonehead, Klutz & Company." While a change of auditors seldom is explained in an annual report, you definitely should find out why this occurred.

Changes in Accounting Policies

You were alerted to the importance of a company's accounting policies in Chapter 12. In this instance, when a company changes accounting policies, and/or the method of applying them, and this has a material impact on the comparability of the financial statements for the periods being audited, an explanatory paragraph is added to the three-paragraph standard report. For example, it has been commonplace in recent years, because of the new FASB ruling on taxes, to see additional explanatory language regarding the treatment of income taxes. A short paragraph is provided at the end of the standard report to the effect that "as discussed in the notes to the financial statements, the Company changed its method of accounting for income taxes in 1991."

This type of nonstandard wording for changes in accounting policies implies that the company has reasonable justification for the change and that the auditors concur. If the auditors do not approve, they would give a qualified opinion because of a departure from GAAP. While changes of this nature do not necessarily fall into the warning-signal category, however, they do warrant further investigation. *Read the referenced note(s)!* Profits can be affected, either beneficially or adversely, by such changes. You should dig into the notes to financial statements section of the annual report to determine the impact of a change in accounting policies on a company's stream of recurring earnings and/or financial position.

Material Uncertainties

Under the new accounting standards, the opinion paragraph is not modified for material uncertainties as in the past. Thus, you will find a three-paragraph standard report, containing an unqualified opinion, with a fourth explanatory paragraph added to discuss the uncertainty. The financial consequences of the circumstances in question cannot always be reasonably estimated by the company or its auditors. This additional paragraph highlights such items, among others, as unresolved lawsuits, debt-agreement violations or the loss of a major customer and/or market share. In those cases where a loss is probable and can be estimated, the loss generally is reflected in the financials of the company and a standard, unqualified opinion is issued.

While technically this type of report is considered an unqualified opinion, the prudent annual report reader should view a material uncertainty paragraph as a definite red-flag warning. Here again, you must read the relevant note(s) to financial statements and make a judgment call on the probability and magnitude of the damage to a company's financial position.

Going-Concern Problems

These circumstances reflect substantial doubt about the ability of a company to stay in business for a reasonable period of time. In similar fashion to the treatment of material uncertainties, going-concern problems are described in an added fourth paragraph to the standard report. Language to the effect that the company has suffered recurring losses, has a capital deficiency, a big contract dispute, etc., and substantial doubt exists about its ability to continue as a going concern will appear in this additional paragraph. The gruesome details will be found in the notes to financial statements section and definitely should be read. Needless to say, you should consider this a rather large black cloud hanging over the company and proceed with caution regarding any related financial or investment decisions.

Emphasis of a Matter

The auditors may wish to emphasize a matter in the financial statements but still issue a report with an unqualified opinion. Thus, an explanatory paragraph is added to the standard three-paragraph report that merely emphasizes a certain disclosure. One of the more common examples of this circumstance relates to a company doing business with other companies controlled by, and people who are related to, the officers of the company. Once again, read the related notes for details, but, generally speaking, this nonstandard wording does not indicate a problem and falls into the benign category in terms of concern.

Qualified Opinions

A number of circumstances cause auditors to use nonstandard language in the opinion paragraph of the auditors' report, thus requiring the auditors to issue qualified opinions. These nonstandard, qualified auditors' reports seriously damage the credibility of the affected company's financial statements, except in the following instance.

In this circumstance of a qualified opinion that should not necessarily alarm you, the auditors qualify their opinion because of a limitation in the scope of their audit. For example, they may not have been able to collect sufficient evidence on the value of a company's investment in a foreign subsidiary. An explanation to this effect and a quantification of the monetary consequence to the financial statements is provided. If the monetary consequence is not material to the overall financial position of the company, I would not be terribly concerned.

You should exercise much more care when considering auditors' reports that

    1. Contain a disclaimer.

2. Are qualified because of a company's departure from GAAP.

3. Indicate a material misstatement of a company's financial position. Auditors will disclaim (not express an opinion) when they have not obtained sufficient evidence to form an opinion on the financials. Departures from GAAP generally mean that a company's financials are misstated, making it difficult to assess fairly its financial position. When departures from GAAP are so material and so pervasive, the auditors issue an adverse opinion that concludes that the financial statements do not present fairly the financial position of the company. In all cases, the often lengthy and scary nature of the language is easily recognized.

□ THE PRICE WATERHOUSE AUDITORS' REPORT FORMAT

Exhibit 13.3 illustrates the maverick approach to the standard format of the auditors' report employed by Price Waterhouse (PW). In contrast to the rest of the accounting profession, PW chooses to use a single, all-encompassing paragraph to express its audit reports. It says the same thing as the others but in a different order and with fewer words. Because PW is a major accounting firm, you will encounter these single-paragraph auditors' reports in numerous corporate annual reports. Do not be confused. As you can see in the exhibit, by rearranging the parts, the message is basically the same as the more conventional approach used by the other accounting firms.

In summary, the management report is nice to see in a company's annual report, but you need not concern yourself with it beyond noticing that it is there. As a general rule, the auditors' report, in its standard form, will provide you with the assurance that the financials in an annual report are a reasonably reliable base for analyzing a company's financial position and performance. The report is not an unconditional guarantee of financial soundness and in no way implies any kind of recommendation for a credit or investment relationship. If you encounter a nonstandard auditors' report, you need to read a little more carefully and exercise some judgment regarding the implications of the information provided. Needless to say, in most instances, a qualified opinion is a clear indication of trouble and warns the reader accordingly.

"Rearranging the Parts"

Introductory Paragraph ●
These financial statements are the responsbility of the Company's management; our responsbility is to express an opinion on these financial statements based on our audits.

Scope Paragraph ▲
We conducted our audits of these financial statements in accordance with generally accepted auditing standards that require that we plan and perform the audit to obtain reasonable assurance about whether the financial statements are free of material misstatement. An audit includes examining, on a test basis, evidence supporting the amounts and disclosures in the financial statements, assessing the accounting principles used and significant estates made by the management and evaluating the overall financial presentation. We believe that our audits provide a reasonable basis for the opinion expressed above.

Opinion Paragraph ■
In our opinion, the accompanying consolidated balance sheets and the related consolidated statements of income, cash flows and changes in shareholders' equity present fairly, in all material respects, the financial position of XYZ Company and its subsidiaries at December 31, 1990, and 1991, and the results of their operations and cash flows for each of the three years in the period ended December 31, 1991, in conformity with generally accepted accounting principles.

EXHIBIT 13.3 Example of the Auditors' Report Format Used by Price Waterhouse

---

REPORT OF INDEPENDENT ACCOUNTANTS

To the Shareholders and Board of Directors of the XYZ Company:

■ In our opinion, the accompanying consolidated balance sheets and the related consolidated statements of income, cash flows and changes in shareholders' equity present fairly, in all material respects, the financial position of XYZ Company and its subsidiaries at December 31, 1990, and 1991, and the results of their operations and cash flows for each of the three years in the period ended December 31, 1991, in conformity with generally accepted accounting principles.● These financial statements are the responsibility of the company's management; our responsibility is to express an opinion on these financial statements based on our audits.▲ We conducted our audits of these financial statements in accordance with generally accepted auditing standards that require that we plan and perform the audit to obtain reasonable assurance about whether the financial statements are free of material misstatement. An audit includes examining, on a test basis, evidence supporting the amounts and disclosures in the financial statement, assessing the accounting principles used and significant estimates made by the management and evaluating the overall financial presentation. We believe that our audits provide a reasonable basis for the opinion expressed above.

Price Waterhouse
Hometown, USA
February 22, 1992

14 | QUARTER-BY-QUARTER REVIEW

☐ READING THE QUARTERLY DATA

While admittedly limited in scope, a few aspects of the presentation of a company's quarterly data in an annual report have some value. Companies are required by the SEC to provide at least two years of unaudited quarterly information, and this is what most of them do in practice. The content generally is confined to the reporting of quarterly results for sales, earnings and per-share earnings and possibly dividend and stock price movement. The illustration of the quarterly data from Lands' End, Inc.'s 1991 annual report in Exhibit 14.1 is representative of many of such presentations, but you will see any number of variations to this format. The information usually is presented separately, but it can appear as part of the notes to the financial statements.

☐ OPERATIONAL INSIGHTS

The sales and earnings figures can indicate the degree of seasonality that a company experiences in its operations. For example, Christmas shoppers obviously give Lands' End a big boost in sales in the last

EXHIBIT 14.1 Quarterly Data—Lands' End, Inc., 1991

(Thousands except per share data)

	Fiscal 1991					Fiscal 1990				
	1st Qtr	2nd Qtr	3rd Qtr	4th Qtr	Year	1st Qtr	2nd Qtr	3rd Qtr	4th Qtr	Year
Net sales	$112,191	$117,088	$145,365	$229,331	$603,975	$108,098	$104,235	$131,574	$201,294	$545,201
Gross profit	43,888	44,738	58,279	99,763	246,668	45,336	42,920	56,424	86,948	231,628
Pretax income (loss)	2,790	(3,608)	390	25,371	24,943	7,586	3,525	9,100	27,059	47,270
Net income (loss)	1,702	(2,201)	238	15,004	14,743	4,703	2,184	5,641	16,543	29,071
Net income (loss) per share	$0.09	$(0.12)	$0.02	$0.78	$0.75	$0.23	$0.11	$0.28	$0.83	$1.45
Cash dividends	—	—	—	3,878	3,878	—	—	—	$3,995	$3,995
Cash dividends per share	—	—	—	$0.20	$0.20	—	—	—	$0.20	$0.20
Common shares outstanding	19,869	19,859	19,489	19,218	19,218	20,050	20,048	20,062	19,881	19,881
Market price of shares outstanding										
—market high	19⅜	17	15¼	17½	19⅜	35¾	32½	31⅛	29	35¾
—market low	14¾	14¾	9⅛	9	9	28	26⅞	26	16	16

The company's fiscal year consists of the 12-month period which begins on February 1 and ends on January 31. For internal accounting purposes, however, the company uses a 52-53 week year. Interim quarterly financial data reflect period end dates that coincide with the internal accounting calendar.

Source: Lands' End 1991 Annual Report. Reprinted by permission.

quarter (November–January) of its fiscal year. If you need an average market price of a company's stock, this is a quick way to obtain this information. Also, examining the range of the stock price will help to point out the volatility of share prices. The dividend record will give you an idea of the consistency of a company's payouts to its shareholders. Finally, I think the most useful aspect of quarterly data is that you can plot the year-to-year quarterly trends in sales and earnings. Unfortunately, because most annual reports generally present only two years' worth of data, it becomes necessary to obtain additional data from previous years' reports to be able to plot three- to five-year trends.

Exhibit 14.2 simulates this exercise for you by using Lands' End's numbers taken from its 1991 annual report. I also have formatted the table to make it is easier to discern the quarter-to-quarter changes and suggest you do the same if undertaking these calculations for your own purposes (figures in millions):

EXHIBIT 14.2 Plotting Year-to-Year Quarterly Trends—Lands' End, Inc., 1991

Sales & Services	1989 (Base Year)	1990	1989–90 Change	1991	1990–91 Change
1st Qtr	$ 91	$109	+20%	$112	+ 3%
2nd Qtr	$ 90	$104	+16%	$117	+13%
3rd Qtr	$109	$132	+21%	$145	+10%
4th Qtr	$166	$201	+21%	$229	+14%
Net Income					
1st Qtr	$ 5.2	$ 4.7	–10%	$ 1.7	– 64%
2nd Qtr	$ 2.6	$ 2.2	–15%	$ (2.2)	–200%
3rd Qtr	$ 6.1	$ 5.6	– 8%	$ .2	– 96%
4th Qtr	$18.4	$16.5	–10%	$15.0	– 9%

Source: Lands' End 1991 Annual Report. Reprinted by permission.

Reviewing and comparing quarterly sales and earnings results is akin to performing a sensitivity analysis on the company's operations, which may provide an insight difficult to detect if you were to rely strictly on annual figures.

15 HISTORICAL PERSPECTIVE

☐ HISTORICAL SUMMARY OF FINANCIAL DATA

In my treatment of the various components of an annual report, the location of this financial summary data is assumed to fall toward the end of the document. As seen so often with the format of an annual report, this is not universally true. Nevertheless, this section is recognizable under one of these generally used titles: Financial Summary, Historical Financial Summary, Statistical Review, Selected or Summarized Financial Data, Five- or Ten-Year Summary, and possibly even Historical Summary of Financial Data.

☐ USEFUL PERSPECTIVES

Once you have identified and located this section, you should be able to understand quite easily its content and usefulness. Generally, you will find five years (the minimum requirement), ten years or eleven years (needed for ten-year averages) of selected income statement, balance sheet, general financial position, per-share, ratio and corporate data. This information provides useful perspectives on a company's financial condition and performance over an extended period of time. You learned back in Chapter 6 that you need to look at more than just two to three years of a company's financials to fully appreciate a company's investment or financial qualities. This summarized information allows you to do this to some extent. The usefulness of this section, however, depends to a great extent on the data selected by the company for presentation.

Four years of Coca-Cola's 11-year Selected Financial Data (1990 annual report) is shown in Exhibit 15.1, which provides you with a typical financial summary presentation. Generally, you will see a fairly complete income statement. Per-share data is a standard entry. The balance sheet data usually is restricted to aggregate numbers such as current assets, total assets, total debt, shareholders' equity, etc. Unfortunately, you seldom see cash flow statement figures. There is little commonality among companies regarding the ratios that are used. Also, very few companies explain the computation of the ratios.

Here again, you are reminded of the calculation of debt amounts discussed in Chapter 8. The choice of the components of many ratios can produce widely differing results as indicators of a company's financial health. Many times, I have been unable to arrive at the ratios presented in a financial summary from the numbers found in the financials in the same annual report. The problem lies in not knowing what specific numbers are used in the computation of the ratio. Because of this experience, I tend not to take the ratios in a company's annual report at face value unless their computation is fully explained. Footnote explanations to the ratios, as seen in the Coca-Cola example, in the financial summary can solve this problem. If only more companies would provide this information! Finally, company data of varying content is provided. Such items as the number of employees, shareholders and shares outstanding, dividends paid and the market price per share are common.

How can you use this information? Depending on the scope of the data presented in the financial summary, you can determine trends in some key numbers in a company's financials. In some instances, companies provide five- and ten-year compound annual growth rates. This is extremely helpful for it allows you to compare, for example, the revenue and earnings momentum of recent years against the company's historical performance. If this information is not provided, you can determine it yourself from the figures in the financial summary.

For example, an interesting article in *Business Week* magazine suggested that investors look for low yielding stocks revealing rapidly rising dividends. Among other factors, the article indicated that a company that has increased its dividends by an average of more than 10 percent for each of the past ten years may be an attractive growth

EXHIBIT 15.1 Selected Financial Data—Coca-Cola, 1991 (Dollars in millions except per-share data)

Year Ended December 31,	1990	1989	1988	1987
Summary of Operations [1]				
Net operating revenues	$10,236	$8,622	$8,065	$7,658
Cost of goods sold	4,208	3,548	3,429	3,633
Gross profit	6,028	5,074	4,636	4,025
Selling, administrative and general expenses	4,076	3,348	3,038	2,665
Provisions for restructured operations and disinvestment	—	—	—	36
Operating income	1,952	1,726	1,598	1,324
Interest income	170	205	199	232
Interest expense	231	308	230	297
Equity income	110	75	92	64
Other—net	13	66	(33)	40
Income from continuing operations before income taxes	2,014	1,764	1,626	1,363
Income taxes	632	571	537	496
Income from continuing operations	$ 1,382	$1,193	$1,089	$ 867
Net income	$ 1,382	$1,724	$1,045	$ 916
Preferred stock dividends	18	22	7	—
Net income available to common shareholders	$ 1,364	$1,702[2]	$1,038	$ 916
Average common shares outstanding (in millions)[3]	669	692	729	755
Depreciation	$ 236	$ 181	$ 167	$ 152
Capital expenditures	593	462	387	304
Per Common Share Data [3]				
Income from continuing operations	$ 2.04	$ 1.69	$ 1.48	$ 1.15
Net income	2.04	2.46[2]	1.42	1.21
Cash dividends	.80	.68	.60	.56
Market price at December 31	46.50	38.63	22.31	19.06
Year-End Position				
Cash, cash equivalents and marketable securities	$ 1,492	$1,182	$1,231	$1,489
Property, plant and equipment—net	2,386	2,021	1,759	1,602
Total assets	9,278	8,283	7,451	8,606
Long-term debt	536	549	761	909
Total debt	2,537	1,981	2,124	2,995
Shareholders' equity	3,849	3,485	3,345	3,187
Total capital[4]	6,386	5,466	5,469	6,182
Financial Ratios				
Return on common equity[5]	39.2%	37.6%	34.7%	26.0%
Return on capital[6]	26.0%	25.6%	21.3%	18.3%
Total-debt-to-total-capital	39.7%	36.2%	38.8%	48.4%
Net-debt-to-net-capital[7]	22.8%	14.0%	18.9%	15.4%
Cash common stock dividend payout ratio	39.2%	27.6%[8]	42.1%	46.0%

[1] *In 1982, the Company adopted SFAS No. 52, "Foreign Currency Translation."*

[2] *Net income available to common shareholders in 1989 includes after-tax gains of $545 million ($.79 per common share) from the sale of the Company's equity interest in CPE and the Company's bottled water business.*

[3] *Adjusted for a two-for-one stock split in 1990 and a three-for-one stock split in 1986.*

[4] *Total capital equals shareholders' equity plus total debt.*

[5] *Return on common equity is calculated by dividing income from continuing operations less preferred stock dividends by average common shareholders' equity.*

Source: Coca-Cola 1990 Annual Report (Partial Reproduction). Reproduced with permission of The Coca-Cola Company.

stock. You can test this concept on any company by using the figures for cash dividends generally appearing in an 11-year financial summary. You will get a feel for this by calculating the annual percentage dividend increase from the four years available in the partial illustration of Coca-Cola's financial summary. Using basic math, you will be able to determine from the figures in the "Cash Dividends" line that the stock's yield on a per-share basis has increased 4 cents (+7.1 percent), 8 cents (+13.3 percent) and 12 cents (+17.6 percent) in the years 1988, 1989 and 1990, respectively.

The financial summary data provides you with an opportunity to analyze the trends in a great variety of ratios and relationships that indicate a company's financial well-being. First, focus on the trends in a few key indicators: The growth rates for net sales, operating income, per-share earnings, dividends, book value, total assets and shareholders' equity. Sometimes these calculations are provided, but if they are not presented, you usually can calculate them from the numbers provided.

You should try a little creative number-crunching on your own. For example, assuming the following indicators are not provided, you can calculate a productivity ratio by dividing net sales by the average number of employees to obtain a sales-per-employee figure. Or divide net sales by the average number of shares outstanding to get a sales-per-share figure to complement the earnings-per-share amount. Often, you become aware of an analytical technique, generally expressed as a ratio, through the financial press or through some educational medium. As you know, no indicator has much value unless it is viewed over an extended period of time. The data provided in a historical financial summary gives you the opportunity to check out a company by looking at five- and ten-year trends in a number of financial and investment indicators.

16 LOOKING FOR EXTRAS

□ CORPORATE AND SHAREHOLDER INFORMATION

As I often have mentioned in the previous pages, corporate practice varies greatly when it comes to the annual report format. This is especially true in the sections generally described as corporate and shareholder information. In many instances, the sections are blended together in one presentation. The informational content is inconsistent and often is found in different parts of the annual report. Two contrasting approaches can be seen by looking at the 1991 annual reports of Quaker Oats and the Modine Manufacturing Company. In the case of Quaker Oats, three distinct sections, including the added corporate social responsibility, are presented that, in the aggregate, run ten full pages. Modine, on the other hand, condenses corporate and shareholder information into two pages. Whatever form is presented, annual report users will find some valuable nonfinancial insights in these sections.

□ WHO'S RUNNING THE COMPANY?

First, let's review the corporate information component. Generally, this section provides information on a company's board of directors and its senior executive management. It also may identify subsidiaries, affiliates, divisions, licensees, joint ventures and locations of manufacturing, distribution, sales and service centers. Depending on the nature of a company's line(s) of business, this latter information gives you an idea of the scope and geographic coverage of the company's operations. For example, in these days of increasing globalization of business, it may be necessary for a company to expand to overseas manufacturing and/or sales and service capabilities to stay competitive. The information on facilities, if provided, would be useful in this assessment.

The board of directors is a body of individuals who are elected by the shareholders to be their representatives in managing the company. Among other responsibilities, they appoint senior management, declare dividends and decide substantive matters affecting the company. For those of you investing your hard-earned money in a company, as well as others with an interest in its well-being, you should be given rather thorough information regarding the qualifications of these individuals. The same can be said for the key players in senior management. There is no question that a company's human resources are the key to its success.

Unfortunately, most companies provide either a simple listing of names and titles and/or cursory additional data for their directors and managers. This form of presentation obviously is not very useful. I like to see photographs of these people, and these often are provided. But more important, what really is meaningful is their ages, terms of service with the company, present professional positions, significant past professional experience, professional affiliations and educational credentials. A company's Form 10K and its proxy statement (see Exhibit 16.1) contains some background information on directors and senior management, but the data required in these reports is not so comprehensive as what I have just suggested.

Take the case of Tyson Foods. Its 1991 annual report lists its board of directors and senior management—no photographs and no background information other than the mention of the individuals' present positions. Neither the Form 10K nor the relevant proxy statement reveals much more. In fact, the meager credentials provided on the members of the board in these documents indicate modest professional achievements for the group as a whole. And yet, the company is one of the world's largest producers and marketers of food products with $4 billion in sales and 47,000 employees (1991 fiscal year). If I were one of Tyson Foods's shareholders, I might wonder whether the board, from what I have been told about it in the company's reports, measures up to the tasks it faces. The point here, as with other companies, is that it is important for you, especially if you are a

EXHIBIT 16.1 SEC Filings and Corporate Reports

Form 10K
Filed annually with SEC

Part I

Item 1: Business
• General discussion of the company's line of business, industry, location and history, including acquisitions • Products—list and description of products and trademarks • Operations and facilities • Marketing and sales • Competition • Environmental and regulatory matters • Human resources (employees)

Item 2: Properties

Item 3: Legal proceedings

Item 4: Submission of matters to a vote of security holders
• Executive officers—Names the executive officers, including their ages and positions within the company and business experiences

Part II
Item 5: Market for registrant's common equity and related stockholder matters—provides exchange listing and quarterly high and low stock prices for at least two years, number of shareholders, quarterly dividend data

Item 6: Select Financial data
• Five-year summary of income statement and balance sheet data

Item 7: Management's discussion and analysis of financial condition and results of operation • Results of operation including comparisons between fiscal years • Liquidity and capital resources • Future accounting requirements • Effects of inflation

Item 8: Financial statements and supplementary data
• Independent auditors' reports • Balance sheets for past two years • Income statements for past three years • Cash flow statements for past three years • Statement of shareholders' equity for the past three years • Notes to financial statements

Item 9: Changes in and disagreements with accounting and financial disclosure

Part III

Item 10: Directors and executive officers of the company

Item 11: Executive compensation

Item 12: Security ownership of certain beneficial owners and management

Item 13: Certain relationship and related transactions

Part IV

Item 14: Exhibits, financial statements, schedules and reports on Form 8K (Provides explanation of material event)

EXHIBIT 16.1 SEC Filings and Corporate Reports (continued)

Form 10Q
Filed quarterly with the SEC

Part I: Financial Information

Item 1: Financial Statements • Balance sheet • Income statement • Cash flow statement • Notes to financial statements • Management's discussion and analysis of results of operations and financial condition

Part II: Other information

Item 1: Legal proceedings

Item 2: Changes in securities

Item 3: Defaults upon senior securities

Item 4: Submission of matters to a vote of security holders

Item 5: Other information

Item 6(a): Exhibits

Item 6(b): Reports of Form 8K

Proxy Statement
Sent to Shareholders

• Notice of annual shareholder meeting that provides location, time and purpose of meeting including planned voting issues • Beneficial ownership—name, address and share ownership data of shareholders holding more than 5 percent of outstanding shares • Board of directors—name, age, occupation, year first became director, year term expires, number of common shares held and percentage of shares outstanding that these shares represent • Standing committees—list of purpose and composition of any standing committees • Compensation of directors • Compensation of executive officers—compensation for the most highly compensated executive officers and officers as a group • Employee benefit plans—list of stock options and pension benefits • Certain transactions with officers and directors—transactions between key employees and the company • Relationship with independent accountants • Other business—blanket statement allowing designated proxies to vote on other meeting issues

shareholder, to appreciate the qualifications of the people who are looking out for your interests.

In addition to the capabilities of board members, you should look for another element in this group. The more outside directors, those not employed or affiliated with the company, on a board, the better. This category of director is presumed to focus unbiased opinions and different business perspectives on corporate decisions. The absence of outside directors, or a token number, may indicate a company overly influenced by the interests of management.

The number of companies with a greater ratio of outsiders to insiders has been increasing in recent years. Timothy Schellhardt reported in *The Wall Street Journal*, March 20, 1991, that "the trend away from the good-old-boy board with insiders loyal to the chief executive reflects the turbulent business environment that confronts directors today— from stiff global competition and takeover threats to depressed market values and difficult restructurings. Directors also realize increasingly that they face serious legal liability if they shirk dealing with such challenges and protecting shareholder value."* Here again, Tyson Foods provides us with a rather egregious example of going against the trend toward independent directors. The company has a nine-member board of directors with only four outsiders, and three of the five insiders are Tyson family members.

☐ USEFUL NONFINANCIAL INFORMATION

The shareholder information section generally provides some standard items that are of practical value to both shareholders as well as nonshareholders. You may see all or just some of the following entries mentioned:

- The company's address
- Its stock symbol and the stock exchange or market where it is listed
- The transfer agent and registrar
- Possibly the number of shareholders
- How to obtain a Form 10K
- Particulars of the annual meeting
- Dividend information
- Identification of the company's auditors and legal counsel
- Mention of trademarks and analyst reports
- Dividend reinvestment and stock purchase plans
- An investor relations contact

---

* Reprinted by permission of *The Wall Street Journal*, © 1991 Dow Jones & Company, Inc. All Rights Reserved Worldwide.

Pay particular attention to the following:

- **Dividend reinvestment and stock purchase plans**—These programs allow shareholders to reinvest their dividends automatically and/or make additional purchases of a company's stock directly, by which the company absorbs most or all of the applicable brokerage charges. If you like the company's investment outlook, these programs are highly appropriate for individual investors as long-term approaches to accumulating capital. Presented with these opportunities, you should thoroughly investigate them.

- **The investor relations contact**—This department, often a person is identified, can be an important source of information for you. If you are a do-it-yourselfer type of investor, do not be timid using the telephone, which is better than writing, to get answers to your questions on any aspect of the company's financials or operations. I have found investor relations personnel to be most accommodating in this regard. If they are not responsive, that may tell you something about the company as well!

- **Form 10K**—See Exhibit 16.1 (on pages 133 and 134) for the content of this document, as well as Form 10Q (quarterly report) and the proxy statement. Many investment education pieces extol the virtues of the 10K over the annual report. Often, however, most of what is reported in the 10K is included in a company's annual report. For example, according to the 1991 Quaker Oats annual report, you can obtain a Form 10K from the company; however, "substantially all information required . . . has been incorporated by reference in the annual report . . . or the proxy statement." If you do not feel comfortable with the annual report presentation, look at the 10K. Otherwise, in most circumstances, the annual report will meet your fundamental informational needs.

- **Analyst reports**—Not too many annual reports come right out and advise you of the availability of these investment research reports, but they are easy to obtain directly from the company, if it has been researched. Simply ask the investor relations department to send you copies. A reference to *market makers* means that these brokerage firms will have produced research reports on the subject company. Written by professional analysts, these reports are very informative. Some commentators question their objectivity if the firm doing the investment research also is pushing the sale of the stock. Biased or not, these reports still are useful. You can request reports from the investment firms, but it is easier to make one call to the subject company to determine what, if any, current investment research is available.

The key pieces of information available in the corporate and shareholder information sections of an annual report include:

- Comprehensive biographical data on the members of the company's board and senior management;
- Information on corporate facilities;
- Advisement, if the company offers them, of dividend reinvestment and stock purchase plans; and
- Identification of an investor relations contact and notification of the existence of analysts' investment research reports.

If a company is not presenting this type of information in its annual report, perhaps it is time that the company be requested to do so. If you are a shareholder of a company that is deficient in any one of these information categories, I strongly suggest that you bring this circumstance to the attention of the company's investor relations department.

17

THE END OF THE BEGINNING

I advised you at the beginning of this book that the corporate annual report comes in a variety of shapes, sizes, formats and, most important, reveals varying degrees of effectiveness as a financial and investment communications medium. Nevertheless, it is this latter quality, its information value, that most informed observers would agree is the annual report's most important function. For users of annual reports, good quality presentations make it easier to discern the risks and rewards of investing in or lending money to a given company. Using the insights and guidance I have provided you in the preceding chapters, however, you should be reasonably prepared to extract valuable clues to a company's financial position regardless of how well, or how poorly, a company tells its story in its annual report.

☐ FOR MORE INFORMATION . . .

My objective in writing this book is to provide you with the fundamentals of financial analysis and investment research as applied to annual reports. You should be reasonably prepared, at this point, to deal with the diversity of these annual presentations, both good and bad. I feel obliged to also inform you, especially those of you who are new to this subject matter, that what you have learned here is only the beginning. Financial and investment education is truly a continuing process. There is a lot more to learn. Also, the fast pace of change, which is particularly characteristic of today's business world, requires that you continually make an effort to stay abreast of new elements critical to fully understanding corporate financial reporting.

Therefore, it is fitting at this juncture to provide you with some recommendations to expand on the basic skills you have acquired so far. As I have said, you should think of the annual report as an elaborate set of financial statements. In this context, numerous resources are readily available to you to continue your financial/investment education.

First, I recommend membership in two organizations: the National Association of Investors Corporation (NAIC) and the American Association of Individual Investors (AAII). While these organizations obviously focus on investing techniques, both have a very strong emphasis on education aimed at helping the nonprofessional individual evaluate a company's financial condition and performance. The annual report as a source of corporate information is the subject of seminars, special publications and articles in regularly published periodicals by these associations.

The NAIC's *Better Investing* magazine is available monthly through membership in the NAIC or by direct subscription. The AAII publishes the *AAII Journal* monthly; it is available only on a membership basis. Information on these organizations and these publications can be obtained by writing the National Association of Investors Corporation, P.O. Box 220, Royal Oak, MI 48068, or the American Association of Individual Investors, 625 North Michigan Avenue, Chicago, IL 60611.

Two publications are produced by professional associations that frequently carry articles on various aspects of financial statement analysis. This material, such as that provided by the NAIC and the AAII, generally is aimed at the beginner to intermediate level of financial know-how. An effort is made, in most instances, to explain things in understandable, nontechnical language. *Business Credit* is published monthly by the National Association of Credit Management (NACM). *The Journal of Commercial Lending* also is available monthly, published by Robert Morris Associates, the association for banking professionals who are involved in lending. Both publications are available by subscription and also can be found in most public and university libraries.

Among the many textbooks used in college accounting courses, which include the analysis of financial statements, there is one book that I have used for many years. The recently revised fourth edition of Charles H. Gibson's *Financial Statement Analysis* (Boston: PWS-Kent

Publishing Company, 1989) is a comprehensive treatment of the subject in a format and language that I think you will find user-friendly. If you are serious about perfecting your financial analysis skills, this book can serve as an encyclopedia for those topics that warrant more in-depth study.

Another favorite book of mine is John A. Tracey's revised edition of *How To Read A Financial Report* (New York: John Wiley & Sons, 1983). The book's title does not do justice to the real value of this work. Its emphasis on the cash flow aspects of financial statements, which has been a neglected topic in books of this nature, is extremely worthwhile reading. Here again, the novice will feel at home with Tracey's easy-to-understand approach.

Finally, this book's bibliography contains numerous sources that have been selected for their appropriateness to readers at the beginning stage of their education in corporate financial reporting. For those of you wishing to go into more depth on any of the subjects dealt with in this book, the books, publications and articles listed in the bibliography will provide ample opportunity to expand on the basics that you have been exposed to in this book.

Now that you are prepped to extract valuable information from an annual report, I have one more suggestion to make life easier for you. For those readers interested in a painless, no-cost method of accessing corporate reports, take note of this tollfree number: 1-800-426-6825. The Public Register's Annual Report Service (PRARS) does just what its name implies. You can obtain annual reports from approximately 3,800 companies that participate in the service. If a company is not registered with the PRARS, it will send your request to the company for a direct response. I have found this one-stop shopping approach to obtaining company information very helpful.

Among the many sources of comprehensive corporate information, the annual report remains, as a practical matter, the one most accessible to the general public. Knowing how to get the most out of an annual report can be a profitable exercise. Obtaining qualitatively good information translates into informed decisions. The more you perfect this skill, the more opportunities you will have to succeed as an investor, bank lender, credit manager, financial planner, investment adviser and analyst or nonfinancial professional. I sincerely hope that *How To Profit from Reading Annual Reports* provides you with one of the foundation building blocks in the construction of your financial education.

GLOSSARY

Accelerated depreciation A method of depreciation used mostly for tax-reporting purposes that results in lowering a company's current earnings, thus lowering its income tax payments.

Accounting period In the context of an annual report, this term is synonymous with a company's fiscal year. The last day of the accounting period is the date of the balance sheet.

Accounting policies The accounting methods employed by a company under generally accepted accounting principles (GAAP) for the preparation of its financial statements. These policies are enumerated in the notes section of an annual report.

Accounting principles The basic concepts and assumptions that accountants use when preparing financial statements. Examples of accounting principles include, among others, conservatism, historical cost, materiality and revenue recognition.

Accounts payable *See* Payables.

Accounts receivable *See* Receivables.

Accrual basis Most companies employ the accrual basis for their financial reporting. Under this process, revenues are recognized when they are realized (goods shipped or services rendered) and expenses are recognized when they are incurred to produce these revenues.

Accruals *See* Accrued expenses.

Accrued expenses A current liability in the balance sheet that records accumulated obligations as of the statement date for such items as payroll, employee benefits, insurance premiums, interest due, rent, sales commissions and, in some instances, taxes.

Accrued income *See* Deferred credits.

Accumulated depreciation The cumulative amount of all depreciation, generally shown as a deduction from the historical cost of fixed assets in a balance sheet or in the notes to financial statements.

Acid test ratio *See* Quick assets ratio.

Acquisitions The act of one company acquiring a controlling ownership interest (generally more than 50 percent) in another company.

Additional paid-in capital This account is a component of shareholders' equity in a balance sheet and records the amount of equity capital paid by shareholders over the amount designated as par value for the company's common stock (a.k.a. capital in excess of par or stated value, capital surplus, paid-in capital and additional capital).

Affiliate or affiliated company This term generally refers to a company that is 20 percent to 50 percent owned by another company.

Allowance for doubtful accounts This amount is management's estimate of the uncollectible amount it expects on its customers' trade accounts receivable.

American Institute for Certified Public Accountants (AICPA) As the name implies, this is the professional organization for certified public accountants. The AICPA has been influential in the development of the accounting profession and generally accepted accounting principles.

American Stock Exchange The second largest stock exchange in the United States, located in New York, also identified as AMEX or ASE.

Amortization A gradual reduction of the value of intangible assets and leasehold improvements on a systematic basis over a given period of time. Amortization also is used to describe the regular, periodic repayment of debt, particularly long-term obligations such as bonds and term loans.

Annual meeting Once-a-year event at which management reports to shareholders on the past fiscal year's results and other matters affecting a publicly held company.

Annual report A formal, detailed record of a publicly held company's financial condition and performance. This report is issued yearly to shareholders but also is available to the general public three to four months after the fiscal year-end.

Asset turnover A ratio that compares average total assets to net sales. This figure is an indicator of a company's ability to generate sales from its asset base.

Assets Everything of value that a company owns, or is due to it, that can be measured objectively. Assets generally are separated into current and noncurrent components of the balance sheet.

Audit The examination of a company's accounting records and supporting data under prescribed procedures by independent certified public accountants.

Audited statements Financial statements that have been the subject of an audit.

Auditors Outside or independent auditors, generally a firm of certified public accountants (CPAs), who will examine a company's financial records according to generally accepted accounting standards.

Auditors' report After auditing a company's financials, the auditors provide their findings in a brief report that is incorporated into a company's annual report (a.k.a. Independent Accountants' Report or Opinion, Accountants' Report or Opinion, Independent Certified Public Accountants' Report or Opinion, Independent Auditors' Report, Certified Public Accountants Report and Auditors' Opinion).

Authorized shares The maximum number of shares of capital stock that a company may legally issue under the terms of its incorporation (a.k.a. authorized stock).

Average cost One of the principal methods used to value the cost of a company's inventory. The average cost method, as the term literally implies, produces a gross profit somewhere between that obtained from the impact on the cost of sales under the last-in, first-out (LIFO) and first-in, first-out (FIFO) methods of valuing inventory cost (a.k.a. weighted-average method).

Backlog The accumulation of a company's unfilled orders from customers, expressed as a dollar value as of a certain date.

Balance sheet A financial statement that lists, as of the date of the fiscal year-end, a company's assets (those items of value it owns), liabilities (what it owes) and shareholders' equity (the owners' interest).

Board of directors A body of individuals who are elected by the shareholders of a company to be their representatives in managing the company.

Bond A form of long-term borrowing by which a company issues a written promise to pay a fixed amount of money on or by a specified date at a stipulated interest rate.

Book value An accounting term for the original cost of an asset, less accumulated depreciation or amortization, reflected in a company's accounting records (a.k.a. carrying value). However, the term also is used frequently to describe shareholders' equity, particularly on a per-share basis.

Book value per share *See* Book value.

Bottom line The financial vernacular for net income—the "bottom" or last line in a company's income statement.

Business combinations Accounting uses two methods to record the acquisition of one company by another—the purchase method or a pooling of interests. The former accounts for a business combination on the basis of the market value of assets of the acquired company; the latter is based on the book value of the acquired company's assets.

Capital Money invested in a business by its owners. Sometimes thought of as just equity. However, there are really two kinds of capital—debt (long-term) and equity.

Capital asset *See* Property, plant and equipment.

Capital employed Synonymous with capital structure, capitalization and invested capital. The term refers to the permanent funds—debt and equity capital—employed to support a company's operations.

Capital expenditure The outlay of money to acquire or improve a capital asset.

Capital goods Fixed assets, particularly machinery and equipment, used for the production of other goods.

Capital invested in excess of par value *See* Additional paid-in capital.

Capital investment An investment in capital goods or capital assets of long-term benefit to a company.

Capitalization Generally used in financial writing to refer to a company's permanent capital—long-term debt and equity. Sometimes referred to as invested capital or capital employed.

Capitalization ratio This measurement indicates the debt component of a company's capitalization, i.e., the extent the company's debt is used in relation to the total amount of the company's permanent capital.

Capitalize Under certain circumstances, a company is allowed to record a cost as an asset (that is subject to amortization) on the balance sheet instead of charging it to the income statement, e.g., deferred charges.

Capitalized lease *See* Capital lease.

Capital lease A lease for capital goods that essentially provides all the attributes of ownership to the lessee company. Accounting conventions, therefore, require that a capital lease be reflected as a fixed asset and a long-term liability in the lessee company's balance sheet.

Capital resources *See* Capital and Management's discussion and analysis.

Capital stock The ownership shares of a company, consisting of all common and preferred stock.

Capital structure Synonymous with capitalization, the term refers to a company's relative amount of long-term debt and equity and these resources' relationships to each other and the assets that they support.

Capital surplus *See* Additional paid-in capital.

Cash The most liquid of assets that appears as the first-line item in current assets in a company's balance sheet. It is money on hand and on deposit in banks.

Cash equivalents A company's short-term, temporary investments for the purpose of earning interest on cash that is in excess of current requirements.

Cash flow This term has several definitions. Generally, these are the funds generated by a company to operate the business, make capital investments, amortize debt and pay dividends. Cash flow originates from a company's operations, financing and investment activities.

Certified Public Accountant (CPA) *See* Auditors' report.

Charge A term regularly employed in financial reporting to indicate an expense in the income statement.

Combined financial statements The combination of the financial statements of separate companies that have common ownership interests. The operative word here, however, is separate. The combined position does not necessarily represent combined credit responsibility or investment strength.

Commercial paper Short-term corporate obligations or promissory notes, unsecured, interest bearing with flexible maturities. They normally are issued by top-rated companies or backed by bank lines of credit that guarantee their liquidity.

Commitment fee A fee charged by a lender for committing to hold a credit facility (a line of credit) available to a corporate borrower over a period of time.

Commitments Companies indicate material commitments, e.g., the future purchase of capital goods or leasing obligations, in the notes to financial statements.

Common stock A unit of ownership in a corporation entitled to voting rights and dividends. As part of a company's capital stock, this is a component of shareholders' equity in the balance sheet.

Compensating balances If possible, lenders attempt to require borrowers to maintain a certain level of deposit balances with them as one of the conditions of a loan or credit agreement. These funds, however, should not be thought of as restricted cash.

Consolidated financial statements Consolidation of the financial positions of the parent and its majority-owned subsidiaries reflects the combined activities of a number of separate legal entities into one economic unit.

Construction in progress A component, which is self-explanatory, of fixed assets (Property, Plant and Equipment) in a company's balance sheet.

Contingent liabilities Potential liabilities not recorded on a company's balance sheet. The most common of these are obligations related to litigation and guarantees (a.k.a. contingencies).

Continuing operations A term often used in a company's income statement to distinguish income of a recurring nature as opposed to that produced by extraordinary events and/or discontinued operations.

Corporate officers The senior executive managers of a company identified by title and name; in some instances, biographical data is supplied. This information usually is included at the end of an annual report in a section presenting general corporate data.

Cost *See* Historical cost.

Cost and profits in excess of billings A current asset usually found in the balance sheet of a company working with a customer on a long-term contract basis. As of the statement date, the company has completed work but not yet billed the customer (a.k.a. cost and estimated earnings in excess of billings).

Cost in excess of fair value of net assets acquired *See* Goodwill.

Cost in excess of net assets of acquired businesses *See* Goodwill.

Cost of sales The cost of producing a company's inventory, i.e., the cost of raw materials, labor and production overhead used to produce finished products. For nonmanufacturing companies, this represents the cost of merchandise purchased for resale. Service companies do not have a cost of sales (a.k.a. cost of goods sold and cost of products sold).

Covenants Conditions placed in a loan or credit agreement by a lender to protect its position as a creditor of a borrowing company (a.k.a. restrictive covenants).

Creditor Anyone who "lends" money to a company—financial institutions, bondholders, investors who buy the issuing company's commercial paper and suppliers of goods and services who extend trade credit.

Credit ratings Formal credit risk evaluations by credit rating agencies of a company's ability to repay principal and interest on its debt obligations, principally bonds and commercial paper.

Cumulative effect of change in accounting policies A special item, not part of recurring earnings, that requires specific disclosure in a company's income statement. As the term implies, a change has occasioned an earnings gain or loss outside the flow of continuing or normal operations.

Current Synonymous with short term, generally meaning less than one year.

Current assets Assets in the balance sheet of a company that are cash or are reasonably expected to be converted into cash within the company's next fiscal year.

Current liabilities   Liabilities in the balance sheet of a company representing obligations that are due and payable within the company's next fiscal year.

Current portion of long-term debt   Classified as a current liability, this is the amount of long-term debt that is due and payable, as of a company's year-end statement date, during the next fiscal year. It is considered a fixed charge.

Current ratio   A basic test of short-term liquidity. This figure measures the amount of current assets that are available to pay current liabilities.

Days sales in inventory   A measurement used to determine a company's inventory turnover.

Days sales outstanding   A measurement used to determine a company's trade receivables turnover (a.k.a. DSO and days sales in receivables).

Debenture   The technical term used to describe an unsecured bond.

Debt   Generally considered to be funds a company has borrowed from a creditor, implying the payment of principal and interest. This is a liability, current or long term, that has a high priority ranking for payment.

Debt issuance costs   *See* Deferred charges.

Debt service   This term refers to a company's obligation to make payment, of interest and principal, on the current maturities of outstanding debt to keep its loans on a current status. In other usage, debt service implies just the payment of interest to keep borrowings current.

Deferred charges   A noncurrent asset representing a cost that has been capitalized, e.g., deferred financing costs (investment banking fees) for a securities placement.

Deferred credits   Generally associated with unearned, accrued or deferred income that appears in a company's balance sheet in the liability section. Deferred items represent the collection in advance for goods delivered and/or services rendered, and rather than owing cash payments to the customer, the company has an obligation to provide the goods or services to the customer.

Deferred financing costs   *See* Deferred charges.

Deferred income   *See* Deferred credits.

Deferred income taxes   A long-term liability, this is an accounting estimate of tax payments deferred because a company is permitted to use different accounting methods for taxes and financial reporting.

Depletion   This is the term applied to the use of natural resources such as oil and gas, minerals and timberlands. As assets in a company's balance sheet, they eventually will be used up. Therefore, as they are "depleted," a loss in value is recorded much like the depreciation of fixed assets.

Depreciation The accounting procedure that allocates the cost of a fixed asset (plant and equipment—land is not depreciated) over its estimated useful life.

Depreciation expense The annual amount of depreciation expense generally included in the cost of sales component of the income statement. In the statement of cash flows, depreciation expense, as a noncash charge that adjusts net income, appears as an addition to cash from operations.

Dilution Refers to the effect on earnings and book value per-share calculations when, over time, the number of shares issued by a company increases disproportionately to the growth in the company's earnings.

Discontinued operations Operations that have been or will be discontinued are reported separately from continuing operations in a company's income statement. The purpose is to distinguish these results from continuing operations and thus improve the comparability of earnings from year to year.

Dividend A dividend is a payment, in the form of cash or stock, by a company to its shareholders.

Dividend payable A current liability on the balance sheet, this reflects a declaration by the board of directors of a dividend to be paid by the company to its shareholders.

Dividend payout ratio A measurement of that portion of net income that is being paid out in dividends rather than retained in the business.

Dividend yield A measurement that provides the yield, as a percentage, on a company's common stock by dividing the dividends per share by the market price per share.

Earned surplus *See* Retained earnings.

Earnings A term used interchangeably with income and profit.

Earnings per share (EPS) Indicates the net income (after preferred dividends) per share of common stock.

Earnings report *See* Statement of income.

Effective tax rate As the term implies, a reconciliation of the U.S. statutory rate and the impact of other taxes and tax benefits, resulting in the effective tax rate for the taxes paid by a company in a given year.

Employee Stock Ownership Plan (ESOP) A tax-qualified benefit plan that provides employees with an ownership interest in their company. There are two types: non-leveraged and leveraged. A leveraged ESOP has balance sheet implications. In this form, the ESOP borrows the money to buy the company's stock, with the company providing or guaranteeing the loan.

Equity The general term used to describe the investment that the shareholders have in a company. This is the difference between total assets and total liabilities, the owners' share of the business.

Equity capital Synonymous with equity, this represents what the owners put into the business as opposed to debt capital that comes from creditors.

Equity in earnings of affiliates The amount of earnings, as recorded in the income statement, that belong to the investor company from the operations of unconsolidated affiliates and subsidiaries.

Equity method The accounting method used for recording the value of those investments of an investor company representing 50 to 20 percent ownership in unconsolidated subsidiaries and affiliates.

Estimated useful life For financial statement purposes, and in accordance with GAAP, the period of time that a company establishes to depreciate a fixed asset.

Expenditure Generally used to describe an outlay of funds by a company for the acquisition of an asset. The immediate effect is on the balance sheet. Later, as the asset is depreciated or amortized, the expense is passed on to the income statement.

Expense Generally used to describe an outlay or accrual of funds by a company to cover costs incurred for selling, general and administrative functions; interest; taxes; and other items affecting the income statement.

Extraordinary item As the term implies, this type of entry in a company's income statement is meant to disclose an unusual or infrequent item that is not part of recurring or continuing operations.

Fair market value of assets *See* Market value.

FASB *See* Financial Accounting Standards Board.

FIFO *See* First-in, first-out method.

Finance company subsidiary Generally a wholly owned subsidiary that exists primarily to finance the parent company's sales to customers. Manufacturers of high-value capital goods often use this mechanism to support their distributors and large-scale sales transactions.

Financial Accounting Standards Board (FASB) Beginning in 1973, the FASB became the primary organization for the development of generally accepted accounting principles. Prior to 1973, the American Institute of Certified Public Accountants (AICPA) undertook this function. The FASB consists of a seven-member board of certified public accountants, academics and representatives of industry and government. Supported by a staff of experts, the FASB conducts research, issues rulings and, in general, is the watchdog for proper financial reporting.

Financial leverage The expression that refers to a company's use of debt as opposed to equity to support its assets (a.k.a. leverage).

Financial statements A company's financial statements generally are considered to be the balance sheet, income statement,

statement of cash flows and statement of shareholders' equity / retained earnings (a.k.a. financials).

First-in, first-out method One of the commonly used methods for valuing the cost of inventory. Its effect tends to maximize earnings.

Fiscal year A company's fiscal year is its business year, usually a 12-month accounting period that does not necessarily correspond to the calendar year.

Fixed assets The financial professional's shorthand for property, plant and equipment (a.k.a. fixed capital, fixed investment or capital assets).

Fixed capital or investment *See* Fixed assets.

Fixed charges Those obligations, generally interest and current maturities of long-term debt, that a company must meet to maintain a good record with creditors.

Footnotes *See* Notes to financial statements.

Foreign currency translation Consolidating the financials of international operations requires a foreign currency translation of financial statements in foreign currencies to the U.S. dollar. The effects of foreign exchange fluctuations are recorded in a special equity account to avoid distortions in reported earnings (a.k.a. currency translation adjustment, translation or cumulative translation adjustment and foreign exchange translation adjustments).

Foreign exchange gains (losses) Buying and selling foreign exchange or taking payment for a sale in foreign currency can produce transaction gains or losses. These are not the same as translation gains or losses and are reported through the income statement as realized exchange gains or losses.

Free cash flow An expression that indicates the amount of cash available after capital expenditures (and sometimes cash dividends) are subtracted from net operating cash flow.

Forms 10K and 10Q For publicly held companies, these are filing requirements of the Securities and Exchange Commission. Form 10K is similar to an annual report but with more detail. Form 10Q contains detailed (quarterly) information on a company's operations and financial position.

Fully diluted earnings Earnings per share expressed after the assumed exercise of warrants and stock options, and the conversion of convertible securities.

Funded debt Technically, that portion of a company's long-term debt comprised of bonds and other similar long-term, fixed-maturity type borrowings. Some definitions simply equate funded debt with long-term debt.

Furniture and fixtures A fixed asset, subject to depreciation, that often is included as a component of the property, plant and equipment account grouping in a company's balance sheet.

GAAP *See* Generally accepted accounting principles.

Generally Accepted Accounting Principles (GAAP) Financial statements are prepared in accordance with generally accepted accounting principles (GAAP). They represent a body of accounting research and precedents and agreed upon standards of financial reporting that have evolved over the years.

Generally accepted auditing standards These standards are characterized by adequate planning, an understanding of internal controls and the gathering of sufficient evidence to prepare an audit report. Audit work is to be performed by competent professionals with an independent attitude. *See* Auditors' report.

Goodwill An intangible asset, goodwill arises from business combinations accounted for under the purchase method. It represents the cost to the acquiring company in excess of the fair value of net assets (equity) of the acquired business.

Gross margin *See* Gross profit.

Gross profit The difference between a company's sales and its cost of sales.

Historical cost The accounting principle that values assets at their purchase price. For example, fixed assets are listed in a company's balance sheet at their historical cost less the accumulated depreciation (a.k.a. cost).

Identifiable assets This term is used in the business segment information note in an annual report to identify those assets of the company that are used by each product line or line of business and geographic area of the company's overall activities.

Income Synonymous with profit and earnings. The terms are used interchangeably to indicate revenue gains to the company.

Income before taxes As the term implies, at this level of the statement of income, the cost of sales, operating expenses, other income/expense and special items have all been deducted from the company's revenues. The only remaining expense is taxes (a.k.a. pretax income).

Income statement *See* Statement of income.

Income tax Generally a major expense item in the income statement. The deduction from pretax income, usually identified with the caption "provision for income taxes," results in net income. The tax entry represents levies by federal, state, local and foreign governments on a company's earnings (a.k.a. federal income taxes and taxes).

Income tax payable This line-item caption identifies a company's current tax liability. It is an accrued expense, but because of its relative importance as an obligation, it usually is stated separately in current liabilities.

Independent accountants' report *See* Auditors' report.

"Industry practice" An expression used by companies to explain their application of an accounting policy that runs counter to general practice but conforms to industry usage.

Intangible assets Noncurrent assets in a balance sheet representing items of a "nonphysical" nature, e.g., patents, financing costs and purchased goodwill. The value of these intangibles is reduced by amortization over varying periods of time.

Intercompany transactions Business transactions that take place within the corporate family and are eliminated in the consolidated financial statements so as not to inflate the numbers of the consolidated entity.

Interest expense Generally, a line item in the income statement reflecting the interest costs on a company's borrowings. This is considered a fixed charge.

Interest income Interest earned by a company on its temporary investment of cash.

Interest rate swap A financial product that companies use to protect themselves against their exposure to debt-related changes in interest rates.

Inventory Generally identified in the balance sheet's current assets in its plural form as inventories. For manufacturers, inventory will consist of raw materials and supplies used in production, work in process and finished goods. Wholesalers, distributors and retailers basically will have a finished goods inventory. Service companies will have little or no inventory, with some exceptions such as transport companies that will have supplies inventory used by the business.

Inventory turnover The number of times inventory is replaced during a company's fiscal year.

Invested capital *See* Capitalization.

Investment in unconsolidated subsidiaries *See* Investments.

Investments This noncurrent asset represents a company's equity ownership in unconsolidated subsidiaries and affiliates.

Last-in, first-out method One of the commonly used methods for valuing the cost of inventory. Its effect tends to understate earnings.

Lease commitments Generally disclosed in a note to the financial statements in a company's annual report that (1) details the amount of assets under capital leases in property, plant and equipment; (2) discloses the present value of minimum capital lease payments, which is the amount recorded as part of long-term debt; (3) indicates the total minimum operating lease payments; and (4) provides the annual rental expense for operating leases for the three fiscal years being reported in an annual report.

Leasehold improvements A fixed asset component of the property, plant and equipment account in the balance sheet. A leasehold represents a right to the use of a property under a lease. Leasehold improvements represent expenditures, which are capitalized, for installations, renovations and remodeling of such property. These expenditures are subject to amortization.

Letter to the shareholders That section of a company's annual report that presents a message from the company's chairman of the board or president, or sometimes both, to the shareholders.

Leverage *See* Financial leverage.

Liability Defined as what a company owes to others—creditors, suppliers, tax authorities, etc. As a section of the balance sheet, it is divided into current liabilities and long-term liabilities.

LIFO *See* Last-in, first-out method.

Line of credit A term that is related to a company's borrowing relationships, generally with commercial banks. This is an agreement that sets the terms and conditions for borrowing up to a set amount of money.

Liquid assets A term associated with the most liquid of current assets—cash, cash equivalents, marketable securities and trade receivables—that can be quickly converted to cash.

Liquidity A much-used phrase in financial reporting that refers to the ease with which a company's assets can be converted to cash. A business is said to be liquid when it holds a high proportion of largely liquid assets.

Listed stock The stock of a company traded on either the New York, American or regional stock exchanges, and NASDAQ, the over-the-counter market. For securities to be considered marketable, they must be listed.

Loan or credit agreement A formalized, contractual arrangement between a lender and a borrower that sets the terms and conditions for borrowing.

London Interbank Offered Rate (LIBOR) The equivalent of the prime rate as applied to Eurodollar loans.

Long term A term used to indicate a period of time that extends for more than one year.

Long-term debt As presented in a balance sheet, this is a long-term liability and an important component of a company's capitalization. Long-term debt represents borrowed funds, usually subject to a formal loan or credit agreement, that are due for payment after one year, usually over several years.

Long-term investments *See* Investments.

Long-term liabilities As the term implies, these are obligations that fall due after one year and follow current liabilities in a company's balance sheet presentation.

Lower of cost or market An accounting term representative of the generally accepted accounting principle of conservatism. As the term implies, the valuation having the least favorable effect on a company's financial position is the one applied. Seen most often with inventory and marketable securities.

Management's discussion and analysis   Referred to as MD&A, this is an important section in a company's annual report in which management comments on the results of operations, liquidity and capital resources for the years under review. This section also should include prospective information on these and other activities of the company.

Margin   The term used to indicate the percentage difference between the selling price of merchandise (sales) and various levels of cost or expense: for example, gross margin (gross profit divided by sales), operating margin (operating income divided by sales) and profit margin (net income divided by sales). All are indicators of profitability.

Market   *See* Market value.

Marketable equity securities   Securities representing ownership of common or preferred stock that are listed, thus providing ready marketability and conversion to cash.

Marketable securities   Securities representing a company's temporary investment of cash in safe, highly liquid instruments for interest or dividend yield.

Market value   The current value of an asset—what it can be sold for on the open market. Often expressed simply as market or fair market value. Its most common application in a company's financial statements is seen with valuations concerning marketable securities and inventory.

Minority interest   This balancing entry will appear in the liabilities section of the balance sheet for those companies with consolidated subsidiaries that are not wholly owned.

Mortgage   One form of long-term debt in the long-term liability section of a balance sheet.

NASDAQ   The abbreviation, which is more recognized and used than the full name, for the National Association of Securities Dealers Automated Quotations. NASDAQ is a computerized communication network that handles the securities transactions of the over-the-counter market.

Net assets   Synonymous with net worth and shareholders' equity. The term implies a modification of the fundamental accounting equation, i.e., assets minus liabilities equals equity, or net assets.

Net income   As the "bottom line" on the income statement, net income represents the earnings generated by the company's operations after total revenues and expenses have been matched.

Net income per share   *See* Earnings per share.

Net loss   The opposite of net income.

Net profit   *See* Net income.

Net sales Represents the value from a company's sales of goods and services.

Net working capital *See* Working capital.

Net worth Synonymous with shareholders' equity and net assets. In financial writing, the term is used frequently to represent the ownership interest in a company.

New York Stock Exchange (NYSE) Founded in 1792 in New York, the NYSE is the world's largest securities exchange with more than 2,000 companies listed (a.k.a. the "Big Board").

Noncash charge An expression used to refer to those expense items in a company's income statement that, as accounting entries, reduce earnings but do not represent an outflow of cash. As such, the earnings reported in the cash flow statement are adjusted, i.e., these noncash charges are added back into cash flow from operations.

Noncurrent Synonymous with long term. Usually applied to those assets of the balance sheet that are of a more permanent nature, e.g., fixed assets.

Nonrecurring An expression used in reference to the sources of earnings in the income statement that are, as the term implies, unusual, extraordinary or one-time events.

Notes payable A current liability in the balance sheet for money owed by a company as evidenced by a written promissory note. Usually represent amounts owed to banks.

Notes receivable *See* Receivables.

Notes to financial statements That section of a company's annual report that follows the presentation of the financial statements. The notes provide additional disclosure of information of critical importance to fully understanding a company's financials (a.k.a. footnotes).

Off-balance-sheet financing An expression that refers to those circumstances by which a company is able to take advantage of debtlike resources, e.g., operating leases, without these obligations appearing as debt on the face of the balance sheet.

Operating cycle This term refers to the period of time encompassing a company's acquisition of raw materials, its production of goods and the collection of its sales. The time span can be measured by adding a company's days sales outstanding in receivables and its days sales in inventory.

Operating expenses Generally considered to be those selling, general and administrative and other costs related to the operations of a company.

Operating income The deduction of the cost of sales and operating expenses from a company's net sales produces operating income.

Operating lease A contract by which the lessor company maintains formal ownership of the property or equipment and grants the use of the property or equipment to a lessee company in return for rental payments. These payments are charged to the statement of income as rental expense. Conservative analysts consider operating leases as off–balance-sheet financing.

Operating working capital A term that refines the conventional definition of working capital by excluding cash, short-term investments and short-term borrowings. Changes in operating working capital items are reconciled in the operations section of the cash flow statement. These changes affect the outcome of a company's net operating cash flow.

Other assets Usually used in the noncurrent section of assets in the balance sheet. A catchall category for miscellaneous assets.

Other current assets Some item(s) that management expects to convert to cash within the next fiscal year.

Other current liabilities Obligations due within the next fiscal year that have not otherwise been specifically identified as accrued expenses or accruals.

Other income/expense Nonoperating items that appear in the statement of income. As income, they could include interest earnings, sale of assets, royalties, dividends, equity in earnings of affiliates and other sundry gains. As an expense, foreign exchange losses, asset write-offs and other miscellaneous charges would be included. If not specifically stated, interest expense may become lost in an aggregate amount or net number.

Other Postretirement Employee Benefits (OPEB) A rule proposed in 1989 by the Financial Accounting Standards Board (FASB) that would require companies in 1993 to record the expense for postretirement health-care benefits on an accrual basis, the way pension retirement benefits presently are handled (a.k.a. other postretirement benefits).

Over-the-counter market (OTC) *See* NASDAQ.

Paid-in surplus *See* Additional paid-in capital.

Par value The stated value on the face of a stock certificate.

Patents *See* Intangible assets.

Payables A current liability representing amounts owed by a company to suppliers for the purchase of goods and services under varying terms of payment. This is referred to as trade credit (a.k.a. accounts payable).

Pension/retirement plans A company's pension plan status is now the subject of a significant disclosure in the notes to financial statements in an annual report. In general, the note will provide a description of (1) the plan or plans, (2) pension expense components, (3) a reconciliation of each plan's status and (4) the actuarial assumptions employed.

"Poison pill" *See* Shareholder rights plan.

Pooling of interests *See* Business combinations.

Preferred stock A form of capital stock that represents ownership in a company. Preferred stock has precedence over common stock regarding its owner's rights to the receipt of dividends and the distribution of assets in a liquidation. It generally carries no voting rights, or only under certain conditions. The dividend rate usually is fixed; if the stock is designated as cumulative preferred stock, any arrears (for dividends not paid) must be paid before any dividend payment is made to common shareholders.

Prepaid expense A current asset representing an advance payment, generally for services and supplies, that is classified as current in the balance sheet.

Present value A concept that measures the value today of a future inflow or outflow of money.

Pretax income *See* Income before taxes.

Price-earnings ratio Much used by the investment community, the PE ratio shows the relationship between a company's earnings per share and its market price per share (a.k.a. earnings multiple or just multiple).

Primary earnings *See* Earnings per share.

Prime rate A base rate used by lenders for establishing interest rates on a company's borrowings. Major money center banks, generally in New York, are the most influential in establishing the prime rate, which is the rate that commercial banks charge their most creditworthy customers.

Profit Used interchangeably with earnings and income.

Profitability A term used to comment on the ability of a company to produce profits. There are numerous measurements of a company's profitability. Some of the more widely used indicators include comparisons of gross profit, operating income, pretax income and net income to net sales, as well as net income to average equity, capitalization and assets.

Pro forma A manner of presentation of unaudited financial information, often employed in the note on acquisitions in an annual report, showing the combined full-year results of the parent and acquired company. It assumes that business purchases are effected at the beginning of the fiscal year.

Property, plant and equipment Commonly referred to as fixed assets, this descriptive phrase is usually the formal term that appears as the account title as a noncurrent asset in the balance sheet (a.k.a. fixed capital, fixed investment and capital assets).

Provision for income taxes *See* Income tax.

Purchase method *See* Business combinations.

Quality of earnings A term that refers to how a company generates its earnings. High-quality earnings are characterized by a company's application of (1) conservative accounting policies; e.g., LIFO inventory, accelerated depreciation and short-term amortization of deferred charges, goodwill, etc.; (2) increased sales from volume; (3) costs that are stable, or better yet, lower than previous years; and (4) the absence in the statement of income of nonrecurring, extraordinary items (gains) that artificially inflate earnings.

Quarterly data Selected financial information on a company's two or three most recent fiscal years, presented on a quarterly basis either as a note or as a separate section in a company's annual report.

Quick assets ratio This liquidity measure further refines the current ratio by comparing those current assets that are cash or cash equivalents and trade receivables to total current liabilities (a.k.a. the acid test ratio and the quick ratio).

Ratios Ratios take absolute numbers from a company's financial statements and convert them into meaningful relationships. Generally, financial ratios are expressed either as a times multiple (x) or a percentage (%). Looked at over an extended period of time and/or compared to other companies and industry averages, they provide insight into a company's financial condition and performance.

Realized exchange gain (loss) *See* Foreign exchange gains (losses).

Receivables A current asset that represents amounts owed to a company that are to be collected within the next fiscal year. Generally, trade receivables, amounts due from customers for the goods and services they have purchased, account for practically all of the receivable amount. A note receivable generally represents the sale of some asset or the conversion of a trade receivable from open account to a note basis (a.k.a. accounts receivable).

Receivable turnover The number of times accounts receivable are replaced during a company's fiscal year.

Reclassifications This term usually appears in the note on accounting policies in a company's annual report. It refers to a common practice of restating certain financial statement accounts in a previous year, or years, to conform with the most recent presentation. This restatement makes the statements more comparable.

Redeemable preferred stock A line item in a company's balance sheet that falls into a kind of no-man's-land between the liability and equity sections. The SEC will not allow preferred stock with mandatory redemption requirements to be shown as part of equity. Conservative analysis views redeemable preferred stock as having more of the characteristics of debt (it is included in long-term debt calculations) than equity.

Registrar The agent, usually a bank or trust company, responsible for keeping track of the issuance and distribution of a company's shares and bonds. The company's registrar is identified in the annual report in the section for shareholder information.

Related party transactions This term refers to the FASB requirement that information on business transactions between a company and its affiliates, major shareholders, investees, officers and directors be disclosed in a note in a company's annual report.

Report of management A statement by management that often appears next to the auditors' report in an annual report confirming management's responsibility for the preparation and presentation of the company's financial statements (a.k.a. Management's Report, Management's Responsibility for Financial Reporting and Management's Report on Financial Statements).

Research and development (R&D) expense An investment in R&D is important for many companies, and they often prefer to highlight these expenses in their income statements as opposed to having R&D expenses buried in a summary account such as selling, general and administrative expense.

Restrictive covenant *See* Covenants.

Restructuring While restructuring can cover a multitude of sins, it often is related to the losses ("restructuring charges" as special items in the income statement) incurred when a company divests itself of poor performing businesses.

Retained earnings An important component of the shareholders' equity account in a company's balance sheet, retained earnings represent profits that have been kept in the business. They have not been distributed (paid out) as dividends but rather "retained" in the company as permanent working capital or to finance fixed investment (a.k.a. undistributed earnings or profits, earned surplus, accumulated profits and retained income).

Return on Among others, there are four "return on" measurements of profitability that tend to appear in corporate financial reporting. However, there is little standardization of usage. These four profit indicators reflect a company's return on assets, capital employed, equity and sales by comparing either net income or operating income to the previously mentioned financial statement elements.

Revenue This term is used inconsistently in financial reporting. Generally, revenues will be a caption in the income statement indicating the gross or total inflow of funds to a company. By far, the most important source would be net sales, to which would be added such nonoperating income sources as interest income or equity in earnings of affiliates. This form of presentation is characteristic of the single-step format for the income statement. In other instances, however, particularly with service companies, revenues are synonymous with sales.

Sale-leaseback An off-balance-sheet financing mechanism by which a company sells a fixed asset, generally property, to another party and then leases it back. A sale-leaseback transaction generates an immediate inflow of cash, and the lease is structured as an operating lease so that the company pays for the continued use of the asset as an expense; there is no debt on the balance sheet.

Sales Some corporate annual reports will employ the term sales without the net prefix. Nevertheless, the concept of netting out allowances, discounts, returns, etc., still applies because of generally accepted accounting principles. Therefore, sales and net sales are synonymous.

Securities A broad term that generally is used to describe government obligations and corporate debt and equity issues.

Securities and Exchange Commission (SEC) The SEC, established as a federal agency by the U.S. Congress in 1934, regulates the securities business and protects the interests of the investing public. Under the Securities Exchange Act of 1934, the SEC was given the ultimate authority for establishing the generally accepted accounting principles for companies whose stock is publicly held. For the most part, however, the SEC has allowed the Financial Accounting Standards Board (FASB) and its predecessor, the American Institute of Certified Public Accountants (AICPA), to exercise this responsibility.

Segment information Many companies operate in more than one line of business. The FASB requires publicly held companies to provide selected financial data on these distinct activities in the notes to financial statements. A note will provide a breakdown of sales or revenues; operating profit or loss; identifiable assets; depreciation, depletion or amortization and capital expenditures by each of the company's product lines or lines of business and its geographic markets (a.k.a. business segment information).

Selling, general and administrative (SG&A) expense A grouping of expenses in the income statement that, in effect, are a company's operating expenses. SG&A expenses generally include salaries, advertising, sales commissions, marketing costs, office expenses, rents, insurance, travel and entertainment.

Senior debt Debt obligations, loans or securities that have a prior claim over junior debt (subordinated debt) and equity holders on the assets of a company in liquidation. Subordinated debt is an example of junior debt.

Shareholder Synonymous with stockholder, a shareholder is the owner of one or more shares of stock in an incorporated business. The shareholders are the owners of a company.

Shareholder rights plan Generally disclosed in a note in a company's annual report with some lengthy, complicated language. A shareholder rights plan, often referred to in the financial press as a "poison pill," is an antitakeover measure. These measures are structured a number of ways but basically give the shareholders the right to buy additional shares, usually at half the price, if their company is the target of a hostile takeover attempt. This effectively "poisons" the company to the raider by greatly increasing the overall purchase price. The rights are redeemable at a token price if management wants an acquisition to proceed.

Shareholders' equity Synonymous with equity, this identifies the ownership interest in a company. On the balance sheet, it is a descriptive title of that section that records the amounts for capital stock, additional paid-in capital, retained earnings, adjustments for treasury stock, ESOPs and/or foreign currency translation (a.k.a. shareowners' equity, shareholders' investment and common shareholders' equity).

Shareholder value A very popular corporate financial communications expression, widely used in annual reports in recent years. Whatever it means, the connotation for the shareholder is meant to be positive and corporate management is dedicated to the cause of providing it.

Shares A company's capital stock is divided into a number of "authorized shares" that represent the number of shares of stock authorized by the articles of incorporation. Shares "issued" or "outstanding" are the next step in the process. A company sells or issues shares to the public, which become publicly traded, in an amount necessary to provide it with sufficient equity capital.

Shelf registration A process, adopted by the SEC in the 1980s, by which a company's securities, both debt and equity, to be sold to the public are reviewed and approved for issuance prior to their actual placement.

Short-term An accounting term that is used to classify assets and liabilities according to when they are to be converted to cash and when payable, respectively. Short-term is synonymous with current when applied to a balance sheet presentation.

Short-term borrowings As the term implies, this generally represents a company's bank debt that falls due within one year of the balance sheet's year-end. Classified as a current liability, it usually is considered part of a company's total debt position (a.k.a. notes payable and notes payable to banks).

Short-term investments These investments represent cash in excess of a company's operating requirements invested in various short-term instruments.

Sinking fund A regular accumulation of a fixed amount of cash or securities in a special fund that is specifically dedicated to pay or redeem an issue of a company's bonds or preferred shares.

Solvency A general term used to describe a company's ability to meet its long-term debt obligations. A counterpart to considerations of liquidity, which focuses on a company's ability to meet short-term obligations.

Statement of cash flows One of the four financial statements presented in a corporate annual report that measures the flow of money in and out of a business.

Statement of financial accounting standards *See* Financial Accounting Standards Board (FASB).

Statement of income One of the four financial statements presented in a corporate annual report that summarizes a company's revenues and expenses for a fiscal year.

Statement of retained earnings This statement reflects the changes in a company's retained earnings, a component of shareholders' equity in the balance sheet, for the period reviewed in a corporate annual report.

Statement of shareholders' equity One of the four financial statements generally presented in a corporate annual report that provides a reconciliation of the changes in the various components of a company's shareholder equity over a three-year period.

Statutory tax rate The rate at which a company's earnings are taxed according to prevailing tax legislation.

Stock appreciation rights *See* Stock plans.

Stockholder *See* Shareholder.

Stock plans Generally appearing as a note in corporate annual reports, this provides detailed information on the incentives a company provides to its executives and employees in the form of stock plans. These could include stock options, stock appreciation rights and stock grants.

Stock repurchase plan A program by which a company undertakes a systematic approach to purchasing its own stock in the open market. Such "buybacks" are what creates treasury stock, which, because it lowers the amount of stock outstanding, figures as a reduction of shareholders' equity in the balance sheet.

Stock split A stock split increases the number of shares outstanding by dividing these shares into a greater number of shares. A company's equity does not change, but a stock's marketability improves at a lower price and a wider ownership base is created.

Straight-line method *See* Depreciation.

Subordinated debt This term describes a form of long-term debt that is "junior," or in a secondary position, vis-à-vis the claim on a company's assets for the payment of its other debt obligations. This means that the other creditors are in a "senior" position, i.e., the repayment of their debt has priority over subordinated debt. Generally considered as "quasi-equity" by financial professionals.

Subsequent events Information that has a material effect on the financial statements for events or transactions, e.g., debt incurred or an acquisition occurring after the fiscal year-end but prior to the issuance of an annual report will appear in a note.

Subsidiary A corporation owned or controlled by another company, commonly referred to as the parent company. Any fraction of ownership above 50 percent constitutes control. Subsidiaries are separate legal entities, but in consolidation, they become part of the parent company's financial statement presentation as one economic unit.

Summary of significant accounting policies *See* Accounting policies.

Tangible net worth A stringent measurement of a company's equity position that reduces net worth by the amount of intangible assets.

Tax loss carry-back and carry-forward These terms describe mechanisms that companies can use to take advantage of tax benefits generated by losses—their own or those of acquired companies—to reduce their tax payments.

Temporary differences This is the expression now used (timing differences was the previous term) to describe the origin of deferred income taxes. Companies are allowed to use different accounting methods for their tax returns and financial statements. For example, the difference between the faster-paced depreciation by the accelerated method (tax return) and the slower-paced depreciation of the straight-line method (financial statements) generates an accounting estimate of deferred tax payments, i.e., a temporary difference. There are other forms of temporary differences, many of which relate to the timing of profit recognition.

Temporary investment *See* Cash equivalents.

Term loan A form of long-term debt, payable over an extended period of time (more than one year, generally three to ten years), provided by a financial institution to a company under a term loan agreement.

Times interest earned ratio A measurement of a company's debt-paying ability that indicates, by a times multiple, the amount of coverage recurring income provides for the payment of interest expense.

Trade A general term that refers to the commercial relationships of a company. The trade prefix used with receivables and payables identifies those transactions occurring within the mainstream of a company's commercial activities. Trade credit identifies the payment terms a company grants to its buying customers and receives from its suppliers. Trade discounts, usually for prompt payment, cut costs to the buyer and accelerate cash flow to the seller.

Trade receivables *See* Receivables.

Transfer agent An agent, generally a bank or trust company, that keeps the official record of the names, addresses and number of shares owned by every registered shareholder. It handles the administrative work related to the purchase and sale transactions of a company's stock.

Treasury stock This term appears as an adjustment entry to the shareholders' equity in the balance sheet presentation of an annual report. Treasury stock represents stock that has been issued (sold publicly) and then subsequently repurchased by the company. Because the stock no longer is outstanding, but has not been retired, holding treasury stock requires a reduction in the company's equity base.

Turnover An expression used by financial professionals to indicate the number of times an asset moves in and out of a business. Generally applied to receivables, inventory and total assets and expressed as a times multiple or in days.

Unaudited The opposite of audited, the term is applied to information supplied by a company in its annual and quarterly reports that is outside the audit conducted by its independent auditors.

Unconsolidated subsidiaries A company's subsidiary operations that have not been consolidated. The parent company carries these subsidiaries in its balance sheet as investments in the noncurrent assets section.

Undistributed earnings *See* Retained earnings.

Unearned income Also known as deferred income, this term describes a company's liability, either current or long term, to a customer for income received prior to the delivery of goods or the rendering of services.

Unrealized gain (loss) A recognition of a change in value in a company's financial statements with respect to the current market value of an asset in comparison to its cost prior to its liquidation. For example, a company may recognize a loss in value (unrealized loss) for an investment in equity securities prior to the actual sale of said securities.

Unusual charges *See* Extraordinary item.

Value In general, value implies the worth of something as measured in monetary terms. For example, a company's machinery assets have a market value—what someone would pay for them. Also referred to at times as fair value. They also have a replacement value—what it would cost the company to replace those same machinery assets. In accounting terms, these two values are considered too subjective to be used for preparing financial statements. Therefore, historical cost, or original cost, subject to depreciation, is the basis used for determining financial reporting values (book value).

Warrants These certificates give the owners of the warrants the privilege of buying a specific number of shares at a fixed price within a specified or indefinite period of time. Warrants are offered as an extra incentive to buy shares when a company is attempting to raise new equity capital. Warrants are considered common stock equivalents when calculating the effects of dilution on earnings and book value per share.

Warranty obligations The ultimate liability for a company's product guarantees and warranties cannot be determined precisely. Therefore, if warranty obligations are material, management estimates an amount for these obligations that is expensed through the income statement and carried as a reserve on the company's balance sheet as a long-term liability and/or accrued expense.

Weighted average of outstanding shares of common stock This calculation is provided for the shareholder in an annual report. It is used as the numerator in the formula for the various per-share measurements, e.g., earnings and book value per share. The weighted average simply gives proportional consideration to the shares outstanding during the fiscal year (a.k.a. weighted average shares outstanding or outstanding shares).

Working capital Simply defined, working capital is the difference between a company's current assets and current liabilities. Working capital is widely used by creditors and investors as a measure of a company's liquidity (a.k.a. net working capital and net current assets).

Working capital ratio A measure of a company's funding adequacy that compares working capital to net sales. This indicates the volume of business a company is conducting on a given working capital base.

Write-down An accounting term used to describe the partial reduction in value of an asset from its cost to a lesser value, e.g., inventory write-downs caused by obsolescence.

Write-off An accounting term used to describe the complete reduction in value of an asset. A write-off recognizes that the asset no longer has any value to the company.

Zero-coupon bond A debt security issued at a deep discount (no interest payments are made) to its face value, thus deferring the payment of cash interest and principal for several years until its maturity.

BIBLIOGRAPHY

Accounting Trends and Techniques 1990. New York: American Institute of Certified Public Accountants, 1991.

"Annual Report Credibility." *Public Relations Journal,* November, 1984, pp. 31–34.

Appleman, Mark. "Annual Reports: Who Needs Them?", *Quaker Quarterly,* June 30, 1987, pp. 6–7.

"The Auditors' Report: The Key to the Annual Report." *Credit & Financial Management,* September, 1985, pp. 14–15.

"Back to the Balance Sheet." *Forbes,* February 25, 1985, pp. 122–23.

Barrett, Katherine, and Richard Greene. "What You Should Be Learning From Annual Reports." *Working Woman,* June, 1986, pp. 38–41.

Bernstein, Leopold A. *Analysis of Financial Statements.* Revised Edition. Homewood, Ill.: Dow Jones–Irwin, 1985.

Board of Directors: Fifteenth Annual Study. New York: Korn/Ferry International, 1988.

Byrne, John A. "This Year's Annual Reports: Show Business As Usual." *Business Week,* April 13, 1988, p. 42.

Cato, Sid. "The Annual Report: Here I Come, World." *Public Relations Quarterly,* Spring, 1985, pp. 17–21.

Corporate Information Committee Report 1990–1991. New York: Association for Investment Management and Research, 1991.

Deloitte, Haskins & Sells. *Summary Annual Reports: A New Option To Improve Shareholder Communications.* Morristown, N.J.: Financial Executives Research Foundation, 1987.

DeNeve, Rose. *Annual Report Trends.* Numbers 1–6. Boston: S. D. Warren Company, 1982–87.

"Do Annual Reports Count?" *Public Relations Journal,* February, 1987, pp. 33–35.

Donnahoe, Alan S. *What Every Manager Should Know About Financial Analysis.* New York: Fireside/Simon & Schuster, 1990.

Downes, John, and Jordan Elliot Goodman. *Barron's Finance and Investment Handbook.* Woodbury, N.Y.: Barron's Educational Series, Inc., 1986.

Drucker, Peter F. "If Earnings Aren't the Dial To Read." *The Wall Street Journal,* October 30, 1986, p. 49.

Evans, Frank C. "How To Read Your Company's Financial Report." *Management Solutions,* December, 1986, pp. 23–32.

Financial Statement Analysis—Simplified. New York: Dun & Bradstreet—Business Education Services, 1987.

Follett, Robert. *How To Keep Score in Business.* Chicago: Follett Publishing Company, 1978.

Forst, Brian. *Power In Numbers.* New York: John Wiley & Sons, 1987.

Fridson, Martin S. *Financial Statement Analysis.* New York: John Wiley & Sons, 1991.

Gahlon, James M., and Robert L. Vigeland. "An Introduction to Corporate Cash Flow Statements." *AAII Journal,* January, 1989, pp. 14–18.

Gibson, Charles H. "Financial Ratios in Annual Reports." *The CPA Journal,* September, 1982, pp. 18–29.

____. *Financial Statement Analysis.* 4th Edition. Boston: Kent Publishing Company, 1989.

Haggie, David. "Annual Report: 9-Point Checklist Gets It Right." *Accountancy,* May, 1984, pp. 72–74.

Horngren, Charles T., and Gary L. Sundem. *Introduction to Financial Accounting.* Englewood Cliffs, N.J.: Prentice Hall, Inc., 1987.

"How Do CFOs Evaluate the Annual Report?" *Financial Executive,* December, 1986, pp. 28–30.

"How To Read Those Annual Reports." *U.S. News and World Report,* February 18, 1985, p. 47.

Janke, Kenneth. "The Annual Report." *Better Investing,* May, 1988, pp. 9–10.

Lipay, Raymond J. *Understand Those Financial Reports.* New York: John Wiley & Sons, 1984.

Loth, Richard B. *The Annual Report Glossary.* Annandale Va.: FIPS Partners, Inc., 1988.

_____. *The Shareholder's Dictionary.* Edwards, Colo.: FIPS Partners, Inc., 1990.

Lynch, Peter. *One Up On Wall Street.* New York: Simon & Schuster, 1989.

Markese, John. "Financial Statements: The Balance Sheet, The Income Statement and How To Interpret Them." Series. *AAII Journal,* July, August and September, 1986., pp. 33–35, 34–35 and 31–34, respectively.

Myer, John N. *Understanding Financial Statements.* New York: New American Library, 1968.

O'glove, Thorton L. *Quality of Earnings.* New York: The Free Press, 1987.

"Professional Investors Critical of Annual Reports, Survey Shows." *Journal of Accountancy,* January, 1985, pp. 28, 32.

Prokesch, Steven E. "The Creative Writing in this Year's Annual Reports." *Business Week,* April 15, 1985, p. 134.

Securities and Exchange Commission. *Management's Discussion and Analysis of Financial Condition and Results of Operations.* Reprint. New York: Sorg Printing Company, 1989.

Server, Andrew Evan. "Cashing In On Cash Flow. *Fortune,* May 23, 1988, pp. 113–14.

Spurga, Ronald C. *Balance Sheet Basics.* New York: Franklin Watts, 1986.

SRI International. *Investor Information Needs and the Annual Report.* Morristown, N.J.: Financial Executives Research Foundation, 1987.

St. Goar, Jinny. "The Footnote Follies." *Forbes,* March 11, 1985, pp. 155–56.

Sullivan, William. "Annual Reports: Finding the Facts You Need." *Better Investing,* June, 1988, pp. 5–6.

Tannenbaum, Jeffrey A., and Lee Berton. "By the Numbers: How One Analyst Scores Big by Finding the Dark Side." *The Wall Street Journal*, August 4, 1987, p. 28.

Tracey, John A. *How To Read a Financial Report*. New York: John Wiley & Sons, 1980.

Understanding Audits and the Auditor's Report. New York: American Institute of Certified Public Accountants, 1989.

Wang, Penelope. "Annual Obfuscation." *Forbes*, May 2, 1988, p. 71.

"What Kind of Annual Do Investors Need?" *Financial Executive*, September/October, 1987, p. 8.

Xerox Corporation. *Reading and Evaluating Financial Reports*. Greenwich, Conn.: Xerox Learning Systems, 1977.

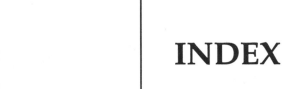

INDEX